CREATIVE WRITING

CREATIVE WRITING

Researching, planning and writing for publication

Alan Jamieson

Focal Press
An imprint of Butterworth-Heinemann Ltd
Linacre House, Jordan Hill, Oxford OX2 8DP

A member of the Reed Elsevier plc group

OXFORD LONDON BOSTON
MUNICH NEW DELHI SINGAPORE SYDNEY
TOKYO TORONTO WELLINGTON

First published 1996

© Alan Jamieson 1996

British Library Cataloguing in Publication Data
A CIP record for this book is available from the British Library
ISBN 0 240 514 3000

Library of Congress Cataloguing in Publication Data
A catalogue record for this book is available on request

Printed in Great Britain

CONTENTS

HOW TO USE THIS BOOK

Creative writing covers a wide range of writing expertise. It includes fictional, imaginative writing — short stories, novels, poetry, drama. It also extends to articles for magazines, newspapers, journals, newsletters — in fact any kind of writing that incorporates research, planning, creativity and style.

This book has been written to help people who as part of their leisure interests or as part of their job need to write in particular structured and yet creative ways.

The book is designed to develop creative writing skills by:

- describing the markets for different kinds of writing
- guiding you through the stages of researching, preparing, writing and presenting your thoughts and views
- assisting you to turn your ideas and material into articles, stories, poetry and novels.

Creative Writing is intended for all people who have an interest in writing: they could be in employment or seeking to improve their skills for social, recreational or creative reasons.

The activities and the assignments are integral aspects of the book. People learn by doing, so there are plenty of tasks and assignments to give you practice. These can be read by friends and commented on, or could be part of a creative writing course.

As you work through the book, we hope that you will discover that:

- Writing is a skill which can be learned and developed like any other skill.
- As with other forms of communication, a writer needs to consider the reader as well as the message. A good writer will think about his or her readers, and will aim to make the message as clear as possible.
- Good written English should be lucid, accurate, varied, and should command the reader's attention. Style, grammar and syntax are important, but writing what you mean is even more important!
- Your writing should be personal; although you respond to readers, you need to find your own 'voice'.
- Writing is hard work. If you want to write well, it is not something to be done in odd moments. Assuming that writing is important for you, it deserves a lot of your time and effort.

How this book is organized

The book has been written as a self-learning guide. You will get the most from *Creative Writing* by:

- reading the text of each unit, in the order presented
- thinking about how the information given can be applied to your

own circumstances and your own writing
- working conscientiously through the activities
- completing the assignments.

Each unit is introduced by a statement of its objectives. Here is an example:

Objectives

Here you will find a brief description of the unit, and a list of objectives. For example, the objectives of Unit 3 are listed as:
After working through this unit you should be able to:

- say why planning is essential as a preliminary to any kind of writing
- plan and organize your own material to suit different purposes and situations
- demonstrate your skill in applying these techniques to your own writing.

Summaries

At the end of each unit you will find a summary of the main points covered.

Activities

Activities are displayed like this, with the icon in the left margin.

Most activities are designed to prompt you to do one of the following:

- give your opinion or views on a topic or a piece of writing
- answer a particular question
- undertake a short creative writing exercise.

It is important to write down your response — after all, this is a book about writing. Additional support on the activity is given immediately underneath, and until you want to compare it with your own ideas you should cover the page with a sheet of paper.

In addition, there are six major assignments spaced throughout the book. These should be attempted as you proceed. You could ask your family or friends to read them, or they could be assessed by a tutor for a course on creative writing.

How long should you spend on each unit?

Creative Writing is a self-learning guide and the amount of time you spend on each unit is entirely up to you. There's no such thing as an 'ideal' length of time to take to work through a unit. You will get the most benefit by progressing at your own pace.

The book is firmly based on assignments, on the basis that you will learn better by writing rather than by reading a text book. So try to complete all assignments.

The times given below are a rough indication of the relative time it might take you to complete each unit including the assignment. Your study can be spread over a period of several weeks, depending on the amount of spare time you have.

Unit	Title	Study time	Assignments
		Time guide (in hours)	
1	Creative writing	2	
2	Engaging your readers	2	
3	Planning, organizing and drafting	2	3
4	Build your skills	3	
5	Writing for magazines	3	4
6	Short stories	3	
7	Writing for children	3	3
8	Autobiography and biography	3	3
9	Plays	3	
10	Poetry	3	
11	Writing for radio and television	4	4
12	Novels	4	4
13	Publishing: preparing for publication	2	

ACKNOWLEDGEMENTS

The author and publishers are grateful for permission to reproduce extracts from these books:

Roald Dahl, *Charlie and the Chocolate Factory*, Penguin Books
David Lodge, *Paradise News*, Secker & Warburg
George MacDonald Fraser, 'My First Book' in *The Author*, The Society of Authors
Roger McGough, 'A Joy to be Old', Faber & Faber
John Mortimer, *Clinging to the Wreckage*, Weidenfeld & Nicolson
John Osborne, *Look Back in Anger*, Faber & Faber
Sylvia Plath, 'Mushrooms' from The Colossus and Other Poems, Faber & Faber
Tom Sharpe, *Wilt*, Secker & Warburg
Muriel Spark, *A Far Cry from Kensington*, Constable
Rose Tremain; *Restoration*, Sceptre Books

UNIT 1

CREATIVE WRITING

Objectives

After working through this unit you should be better able to:
- describe people who fit the definition of 'creative writers'
- say why some people are keen to write
- make an attempt at defining what creative writing is
- describe some possible markets for creative writers
- describe in general terms some of the skills that are needed.

Why write?

'Creative writing' is a phrase that carries the atmosphere of excitement. It conjures up the thrills of being a best-selling author, of promotional tours around the UK and beyond it, of publishers' lunches, film rights and fat royalty cheques.

That could be the glamour side of creative writing. It is (or was) the world of Jackie Collins, Ian Fleming, Jilly Cooper, John le Carré. But they are in a small minority of writers — a *very* small number. There's a large group who write well but don't achieve fame. Their short stories, biographies, poems, novels, travel books, cookery books, magazine articles and so on may be published and may earn a pleasing fee or royalty but the pleasure is largely in being an author and not in fame and fortune.

Then there's a third group — those people who never manage to persuade a publisher to accept their work. Their number is probably the greatest — unknown, unsung and yet hard-working people who find writing a pleasure, not a chore, and who stick to it, regardless of publishers' rejection slips.

But by far the largest group of 'creative' writers are people who work in commerce, business, industry, central government offices, local government offices and for all kinds of companies, large and small. From time to time they — and that is likely to include you — have to write 'copy' for a newsletter, a business letter, an internal memo, a report or a document to promote the organization — a brochure, a press release, a few lines as a caption to a photograph, and so on.

Then there is a substantial group of people who don't yet have a job which requires the skills of creative writing. But they'd like to have the opportunity to write, if only they had the chance. This book and course is for them, too, to assist them in developing the skills of writing in the hope, if not the expectation, of one day being a 'creative writer'.

Activity

What do you think are the main **markets** for creative writing? As with all Activities, write down your answer **before** moving on.

Markets

The market for writers is huge. Possible sources for stories and articles are these:

- in Britain alone there are over 900 daily, Sunday, weekly and regional newspapers
- there are about 10 000 UK magazines, some appealing to general consumer interests (such as 'women's' magazines); others catering for a particular hobby or sport (golf, tennis etc); others with a vocational emphasis (engineering, building, fashion); and so on
- newsletters produced by clubs and societies for their members
- regional or local publications (magazines, interest groups' publications)
- other substantial markets for creative writing are books, radio, television, theatre, films
- then there are the publications of commercial (and non-commercial) organizations such as brochures, press releases, catalogues, manuals, etc.

Different kinds of writing

We could now make an attempt to define what is creative writing.

It could be described as original material produced (and it could be illustrated) to inform and/or entertain people. The material is likely to be written, but in these days of electronic forms of communication, the medium could be computer disk, audio tape, video or film.

Activity

The reasons why some people are keen to write are not too difficult to define. Money has to be one factor. A feeling that you have something to say is another. A wish to tell a story is a third. There are other reasons. List some of the reasons why you think people want to write. Then explain the factors that motivate you personally.

The answer should begin with the reasons suggested above — a fee or a royalty cheque; giving expression to an inner need; part of your job as a writer or editor of a newsletter, and so on. Your own motivation may be a combination of these or a single factor. To express your views in writing and in your own personal terms is the first test in this course book on creative writing.

The skills of a creative writer

What skills do you think are needed to be an effective and successful writer?

First, you feel you have something to say. You have an idea, or a different view of events from the accepted norm, or you feel a bubble (or stream) of words that must be expressed. In short, you are passionate in two senses, one to express ideas, views or feelings, and second, to write about them.

Next, skill with words. Unless your writing is to be for private view only, you have to address and stimulate a reader (better still, more than one reader!). So you must develop these skills by practice and persistence.

Skill with words does not mean the excessive use of them. Brevity and choice of words are more likely to be effective than prolixity.

Style is a personal response to language. It is a writer's deepest discipline and response. Style is the means of conveying information, emotion, events, meaning and attitude. It expresses, too, a writer's viewpoint, that is the particular stance one takes about people, or history, or current events. People develop a particular style of writing that is their unique voice. Style can be copied but a writer would not be comfortable in doing so. The reason is that one's style is unique to yourself, cultivated but not copied.

Some famous writers have their own recognizable style. To pick out some famous examples — Ernest Hemingway's terse action-man writing was copied by thousands of imitators but nevertheless remained unique; Evelyn Waugh's acerbic and polished wit provides a nice contrast in styles. You will have your own favourites and from your reading of other people's work you will eventually find a style — a 'voice' — that is your own.

Creativity

If we knew exactly 'how to write' and could use these skills successfully, we would all be rich and famous. Creativity is largely inspirational, and it cannot be taught. However, creativity is also based on hard work and the exercise of real skills, real writing skills.

Disciplines

In order to organize and practise these skills effectively, a writer needs to observe some personal disciplines. Among them are the ability to organize, plan, carry out research, check and double-check.

Activity

What would be say are some of the **disciplines** needed by a writer?

Some of the **personal** disciplines that are needed are

- knowledge of how to write correct English
- managing one's time to accomplish tasks
- developing writing techniques such as sequencing, story-telling, explanation, dialogue, pace
- researching a topic thoroughly to avoid factual errors
- presenting one's own writing effectively to engage the interest of the reader.

My first book

The Author, the journal of The Society of Authors, has a regular series on 'My First Book' written by members of the Society. This is one of the series, written by George MacDonald Fraser, the author of the Flashman novels, among others.
First, read the article.

MY FIRST BOOK
George MacDonald Fraser

My first book — not counting 'The Ten Sacred Feathers of Pontiac', written when I was nine, running to sixteen pages and confiscated by an unsympathetic maths master round about the time of the Nazi book-burnings of the 1930s — was begun in a moment of pique in 1966. I was deputy editor of the *Glasgow Herald*, then controlled by the late Hugh Fraser, Lord Allander, a genial brigand famous for his takeover of Harrods. He made me acting editor for three heady months but, despite the fact that he was a fellowclansman and called me 'Namesake', I was not confirmed in the editorial chair. Feeling thoroughly miffed, and faced with twenty dull years as deputy, I decided that I had better try to write my way out of newspapers before I got any older. The result was *Flashman*, written in two-hour stints at the kitchen table when I came home from work at midnight, in those silent small hours which daily newspapermen usually spend yawning their way through the first edition. I began with no idea of plot, just a character, courtesy of Thomas Hughes, and a starting-point, Flashman's expulsion from Rugby at the dawn of the Victorian era. After a few weeks and immense consumption of tea, toast, and cigarettes, it was half-finished, and then I fell down a waterfall on holiday in the Lake District, broke my arm, couldn't type for a time, and forgot about it — until my wife asked if she could see what I had written. I dug it out, and her reaction was such that I set to again and finished it. Total writing time, about ninety hours, no revisions; it exists in book form exactly as I wrote it, except for one altered line and a title change from *The Flashman Papers* to *Flashman*.

That it achieved publication still strikes me as a minor miracle. In the two years after completion it was rejected by about a dozen publishers in Britain and the US (one American house didn't like the character's name, another wanted the first half re-written, none appeared to have heard of *Tom Brown's Schooldays*). I was ready to give up, but my wife insisted I keep trying, and then I remembered a literary agent with a Highland name: John Farquharson. Scots have a tremendous faith in their Mafia. So off went the battered heap of copy paper yet again, and after a further half dozen refusals it came to rest in the Dickensian offices (now no more, alas) of Herbert Jenkins. They seized on it with an eagerness that took me flat aback and put it into type as it stood. Arthur Barbosa painted the first of his superb jackets, and I banked my advance (£300, as I recall, and the first foreign rights sold to Finland), and threw myself at my typewriter and the sequel, of which there have been eight so far. I also took a deep breath, resigned from newspapers, and hoped I could make it as a full-time writer.

People are kind enough nowadays to marvel that so many publishers rejected that first book; they suggest that anyone in his right mind would have accepted it. I don't agree; for one thing, it did not turn out to be a best-seller (not as I understand the term, anyway, which applies to the blockbusters of the Macleans and Archers and Forsyths). For another, it is easy to be wise after the event, and there is a huge difference, even for an experienced reader, between a printed book and a mouldering typescript that looks as though it's been lost for years in an Egyptian sub-post office; the former has the authority of publication behind it (well, obviously *someone* has liked it), the latter hasn't a friend in the world.

So I can't blame any publisher for turning it down; having discovered, as a former literary features editor, that I had no idea what would please the reading public, I can even sympathise. It isn't a conventional novel, purporting as it does to be a Victorian memoir complete with introduction and footnotes, written in the vernacular, and impossible, I imagine, to assess or classify in marketing terms. That it got into hard covers at all is due to my wife's unwavering belief in it, George Greenfield's persistence in sending it to publisher after publisher, and the enthusiasm of that happy band at Herbert Jenkins — Tony Samuel, Leopold Ullstein, Richard Wadleigh, and especially Christopher MacLehose, who has been my publisher ever since, whatever the name of the firm. It seemed to me then, and still does, that Jenkins took it not because they saw its commercial possibilities, but because they liked reading it. There are such publishers.

Pure, old-fashioned luck played its part, too, not least in timing. *Flashman* would never have found a publisher twenty years earlier, of that I'm sure. Now, a little more than twenty years after — twenty years in which literary taste, publishing, and public attitudes have changed a good deal — I wonder if that manuscript, cracking at the edges and turning yellow, would find a home today? I don't know; I'm just thankful that it went out in the 1960s, not in the 1990s. Mind you, to go from the ridiculous to the sublime, would a modern publisher jump at *Pilgrim's Progress*, or a producer at *Macbeth*? I only ask the question; I wouldn't presume to answer it. But we agree, timing is all-important.

No one who remembers their first book's acceptance needs to be told that, whatever Dr Johnson may have said, the real rewards have nothing to do with money. For me there have been three beyond all others where *Flashman* is concerned. The first was the sound of my wife laughing in the next room. The second was the approval of P. G. Wodehouse. And the third happened when a film director with whom I was having dinner in a London restaurant called me away from the table to introduce me to a stoutish, bright-eyed old gentleman who was passing by. My name, of course, meant nothing to him, but when the book's title was mentioned he beamed and cried: 'Oh, *Flashman*!', and I realized I was shaking hands with Charlie Chaplin.

© George MacDonald Fraser, 1995

Activity

Give your view
Having read it, what do you think? Is it a good article? If so, why? Or didn't you like it? If so, why not?
In a few lines, give your own critical views of this article. Look for clues in the text and list them or describe them in your analysis.

A flashy story

Were you impressed? You should be — this is very clever writing. For example:

1   The author immediately captures the reader's attention by telling a story about an eccentric millionaire businessman, Hugh Fraser, Lord Allander, once the owner of Harrods.
2   Attention having been grabbed, interest is aroused and maintained by the continuing tale of how his first novel came to be written and published, despite many rejections.
3   The article is cleverly paced, told in the first person, punctuation marked by elisions (don't, can't, I'm) to make it seem informal and personal.
4   There's name-dropping of the famous throughout the copy, with the characters outlined in very few — but very effective — words.
5   There's evidence of careful planning and drafting (later themes in this course book) and a final bite in the story of the last six lines.
6   And what of the reader? Well, if you haven't read any *Flashman* novels, aren't you tempted to try one now that you have sampled this simple, straightforward and very effective style of writing?

Review activity

This is the first review activity on creative writing. Before you start on your own writing, we want you to select and analyse an example of someone else's work. This task asks you to select, read, think about and write about other people's writing.

Look through magazines, books, newspapers, newsletters or any other publication. Select one example of what you consider to be an effective piece of work. It could be a whole article, or a chapter from a book, or even a few paragraphs. Cut out your selected piece or photocopy it and send it to your tutor with your analysis.

What you have to do is to write briefly on your selected item, explaining why you made this choice and why you like it or think it is a skilful piece of work. In your analysis, you might (if appropriate) pick on these aspects:

1 Its **title** (does the title do anything to attract or stimulate the potential reader?).
2 The possible **readership** (who do you think the writer has in mind as possible readers?).
3 Is there a particular **theme or message** or story? If so, what is it?
4 What are the **writing skills** that you can detect and admire?
5 What was your **response**, as the reader?

These points may help you to channel your views or ideas on why it is effective. Of course, you may have an entirely different set of ideas or suggestions to make.

Summary

In this unit we have:

- reflected on some of the reasons why people take up creative writing
- thought about some possible markets
- considered the range of skills needed by writers
- discussed the first approach to writing by a famous author.

UNIT 2

ENGAGING YOUR READERS

Objectives

After working through this unit you should be able to:
- explain why writers should think hard about the needs and responses of potential readers
- make an attempt to judge the anticipated readership of selected copy
- see how authors adapt their style to meet the needs of readers.

A private view

It is perfectly possible to write only for yourself. Many people write stories and articles that are never shown to anyone. There are all kinds of reasons for this shyness — possible personal embarrassment; lack of confidence; anxiety at other people's reactions; writing as personal therapy, and so on.

For all — or one — of these (and other) reasons, it is perfectly acceptable to write only for yourself. After all, once you put pen to paper or fingertips to a word processor, you are revealing a lot about yourself — your views, opinions, life-style, frailties and strengths. Most people prefer to keep their inner personal qualities hidden or disguised. For writers who do not have the confidence or wish to let others into their private world, a diary or exercise book kept in a locked drawer is perfectly acceptable. You may be such a writer, someone who wants to improve their skills but has no intention of allowing anyone else into their secret world.

Open to question

On the other hand, there are writers who expect, or at least hope, that people will read their work and be informed, persuaded or entertained by it.

This means that you should think quite hard about your **readers**. Who are they, these mysterious, unknown people? Advertisers call them 'the target audience'. Unless you are going to be entirely selfish about what you write, some thought should be given to them.

Activity

Here are two extracts which show that authors have different views of their readers. What differences are there between them?

1 'Life in this little resort is, not surprisingly, centred around the beach which is one of the best in Sardinia. The wide, curving bay of fine sand is lapped by incredibly clear water. Around the headland lies a further choice of beautiful sandy coves, and the views of distant islands off-shore and the serrated mountain peaks inland are among the loveliest on this coastline.

Good Sardinian cuisine and wonderful beaches draw people back to Sardinia. By boat you can explore the little islands with their spectacular white beaches and there are lovely walks to be enjoyed in the hills. The resort is small and walking is the best way to enjoy the resort. However if you wish to explore the stunning coastline nearby or try a different restaurant every night, a car is recommended as public transport is extremely limited.'

2 'I always hated holidays, even as a kid. Such a waste of time, sitting on the beach, making sandpies, when you could be at home doing some interesting hobby. Then, when I got engaged, we were both students at the time, my fiancée insisted on dragging me off to Europe to see the sights: Paris, Venice, Florence, the usual things. Bored the pants off me, till one day, sitting on a lump of rock beside the Parthenon, watching the tourists milling about, clicking their cameras, talking to each other in umpteen different languages, it suddenly struck me: tourism is the new world religion. Catholics, Protestants, Hindus, Muslims, Buddhists, atheists — the one thing they have in common is they all believe in the importance of seeing the Parthenon. Or the Sistine Chapel, or the Eiffel Tower.'

'I'm doing to tourism what Marx did to capitalism, what Freud did to family life. Deconstructing it. You see, I don't think people really want to go on holiday, any more than they really want to go to church. They've been brainwashed into thinking it will do them good, or make them happy. In fact, surveys show that holidays cause incredible amounts of stress.'

'These people look cheerful enough,' said Bernard gesturing at the passengers waiting to board the flight. There were now quite a lot of them, as the time of departure neared: mostly Americans, dressed in garish casual clothes, some in shorts and sandals as if ready to walk straight off the plane on to the beach. There was a rising babble of drawling, twanging accents, loud laughter, shouts and whoops.

'An artificial cheerfulness,' said Sheldrake. 'Fuelled by double martinis in many cases, I wouldn't be surprised. They know how people going on vacation are supposed to behave. They have learned how to do it. Look deep into their eyes and you will see anxiety and dread.'

'In 1939 a million people travelled abroad; last year it was four hundred million. By the year 2000 there could be six hundred and fifty million international travellers, and five times as many people travelling in their own countries. The mere consumption of energy entailed is stupendous.'

'My goodness,' said Bernard.

'The only way to put a stop to it, short of legislation, is to demonstrate to people that they aren't really enjoying themselves when they go on holiday, but engaging in a superstitious ritual. It's no coincidence that tourism arose just as religion went into decline. It's the new opium of the people, and must be exposed as such.'

Readers beware

What differences did you spot?

You were asked to think of the **readers**. The first extract is clearly from a travel brochure; the readership is anyone contemplating a holiday to Sardinia. It's a fine example of a copywriter's art and certainly qualifies as 'creative writing'. The reader is pampered and tempted: the heavy use of adjectives (count them up — how many are there?); the superlatives (best, wonderful, loveliest, stunning), and the use of adverbs (incredibly, lovely etc) and the appeal to the imagination all combine to tempt the reader. Thus, **style** is important. But the copy is bland; it could describe lots of places. And the disadvantages of summer Sardinia — the heat, relentless sunshine, separation from the mainland's sight-seeing alternatives — are not mentioned. To counter the impression of isolation, 'a car is recommended'. Put another way, a car is essential.

The second extract is from a novel. The theme is the same — tourism. But a different assumption is made about the **reader**: he or she is assumed to be intelligent and knowledgeable, as indicated in the cultural references to Marx, Freud, the Sistine Chapel and religion. The author hopes to engage the reader's mind by suggesting two startling ideas: that tourism has replaced religion and that people don't really want to go on holidays which 'cause incredible amounts of stress'. The writer's **style** is cleverly effective: amusing, sharply perceptive and intelligent.

If you would like to extend your reading of these examples, holiday brochures provide good (and bad) examples of copywriters' creative skills. The novel is *Paradise News* by David Lodge, published in paperback by Penguin.

Activity

Choose any three examples of published writing done for different purposes. As you see, we define 'creative writing' in a wide sense; we assume that all writing is creative whether it is fictional or non-fictional. This means that newspaper and magazine articles, letters, biographies, brochures, reports and other materials are 'creatively' constructed.

What you have to do is to look at several examples of writing and choose three. Photocopy each selected item and then analyse in your own words how the writer views the **reader**, and secondly how the **style** is set to reflect the needs of the reader. You could choose effective pieces of writing, or to sharpen your own critical judgement, choose one or more examples of patronizing, weak or ineffective writing.

Doing it with style

1 Which of these aspects of writing applies to the three examples selected by you?

    (a) The reader is assumed to be intelligent (or the reverse)

    (b) The reader is stimulated (or bored)

    (c) The style matches the topic and the anticipated reader.

2 Explain, with examples, how the writing is skilfully (or clumsily) constructed to catch, maintain and engage the reader's attention. For example, look at sentence lengths; paragraphing; the use of dialogue; the use (and possible abuse) of adverbs, adjectives, superlatives.

3 Are there any further criticisms (or approving comments) you would like to make about the purposes, planning, language, syntax (grammar and sentence-construction) and general impact of these pieces?

Review activity

This is the first of your personal activities and assignments on creative writing. Later assignments ask you to write for different purposes and audiences. This task is entirely your own choice and asks you to make your own first attempt at writing. You may already have a story, an article, a chapter of a book or some other piece of personal writing that you would like to present. However, it might be best to write a new piece or re-work your previous ideas in order to present a fresh view, having thought about the advice given so far, on matching copy to the needs of readers and devising a style that is appropriate.

Your work should be no more than 800 words. You should think about and implement these factors:

1 **Title** — it could be personal; descriptive; informative. Whatever it is, it is your choice and personal so choose it with care.

2 **Who** is it for? Do you have a view, an opinion, of the potential readers?

3 What is the main **theme**? It may not have a distinctive theme, but it is necessary to decide whether or not you are going to leave the reader in doubt about the theme or be clear about it.

4 At this early stage, think about and **plan** your writing beforehand to ensure it has a **sequence** of episodes or ideas that carry the reader through your piece, maintaining his or her interest to the end.

5 Then, having done this preparation, write it.

You could ask members of your family or friends to read this copy and comment on it.

Summary

In this unit you have looked at some examples of how established writers first grappled with their trade. In particular, you have considered:

- whether to write for private reasons or to seek publication in commercial markets
- the response of readers.

In addition, you should have taken the opportunity to compose your first piece of creative writing.

UNIT 3

PLANNING, ORGANIZING AND DRAFTING

Objectives

After working through this unit you should be able to:
- say why planning is essential as a preliminary to any kind of writing
- plan and organize your own material to suit different purposes and situations
- demonstrate your skill in applying these techniques to your own writing

Planning

It is possible to pick up a pencil or pen (or use a typewriter) without planning. There is a form of composition known as 'stream of consciousness' where authors allow a flow of ideas and words to run freely. At a more modest level, writing a letter to family or friends is a similar technique. Some people find this easy and can write page after page in this way. However, you either need a lot of confidence to be able to write in this freeflow manner, or you plan in your head as you proceed: this is a startling intellectual gift not possessed by many people.

Most of us need to **plan**. At its simplest level, this could mean thinking of:

    (a)   a beginning
    (b)   a middle
    (c)   an end.

Immediately, questions are posed. As you know, all communication has a message that is passed from originator/author to receiver/reader. Should the message be at the start, in the middle, at the end?

The answer isn't obvious. Some writers begin with 'the end' — an episode (such as a murder in a crime story, a marriage in a Barbara Cartland novel, the winning goal in a sports report) — and then go to the beginning and middle. Other authors like the flashback method of narration where beginning, middle and end are deliberately mixed up.

But these are the exceptions. Let us play safe by assuming that planning means, first of all, telling a story in sequence.

ACTIVITY

Think about and then write down the various stages in planning a piece of writing. You can do this by completing the box.

Sequence	Planning	An example of planning is. . .
1	Deciding on the major theme or topic	Write it down
2	Roughly deciding on how many words (or pages) will be needed (or are allowed by an editor)	Decide on a number
3	Decide on how many chapters (or paragraphs for an article) are required	
4		
5		
6		

The planning stage

Your answer could follow these stages:

Stages	Sequence
1	Deciding on the theme or topic
2	Fixing on an anticipated page or word count and chapters or paragraphs
3	Thinking about the content and sequence of what you intend to write
4	Setting out, in brief, the sequence of ideas or episodes from an introduction or starter (the beginning), through the middle stages to a conclusion (end)
5	Deciding on whether this sequence will be interrupted or varied by alternatives to the start, middle, end logical format (such as the use of 'flashbacks')
6	Planning the research required to ensure factual correctness of an article or story by investigating and reading the books needed
7	Carrying out this research and making notes
8	Jotting down the first stages of the plot or the sequence of ideas for an article.

If all of these procedures are followed, you should be in a more confident position to start writing your copy. Planning in this way also gets words down on paper or on the WP.

The contemplation of a blank sheet of paper is an author's nightmare: by following the planning schedule that is suggested here, at least some words are written, thus breaking through the paralysis that afflicts all writers at some time in their career.

Activity

Take an example. Suppose you are a member of a club. It could be a sports club, or a social, educational or leisure club. The editor of the club newsletter asks you to write an amusing article about one of the club's activities that occurred recently. It could be an event, a competition, an outing, a dinner or some other event.

You have to devise, plan, write and illustrate (perhaps with a line-drawing, perhaps a photograph) an 800 word article.

Follow the sequence of thinking, planning and constructing an outline of the article. You don't need to write it in full (but you can if you wish): the task in this activity is to plan it.

Constructing the text

1   A good title or an effective headline can immediately catch people's attention. Do you have one?
2   The first sentence can make or break a story or article. It captures (or loses) the reader's attention immediately. Do you have a smart starter?
3   In 800 words you'll need to paragraph the text— do each of your paragraphs have a separate topic or theme, leading on from the previous one? This adds to pace and helps to maintain the sequence of events or ideas.
4   Is there a beginning, middle, end — or a variation on the three components?

A writer's mnemonic

Professional journalists employ all kinds of skills and tricks to catch and hold a reader's interest. Creative writers can learn a lot from journalists whose daily trade is the effective use of words. Indeed, many journalists have become best-selling novelists, travel, sport and cookery writers because they have adapted their skills and used their knowledge to suit different circumstances and audiences.

Journalists rarely observe rules. However, there is a mnemonic device called AIDA which deliberately or instinctively they use. AIDA aids the memory and concentrates the writer's skill by applying

A:	arousing	*Attention*
I:	sustaining	*Interest*
D:	stimulating through	*Design*
A:	prompting	*Action*

AIDA is, as you might have detected, closer to an advertising account executive's objectives but the discipline can also apply to a novelist or magazine journalist. If a novelist cannot catch people's attention, maintain it through 300 pages, make the plot and characterization (another definition of design) work, and provoke and hold the avid reader's attention, then the novelist won't be very successful and rejection slips will no doubt mount up.

Apply the AIDA principle: it may not always be appropriate but as an exercise it provides a frame for one's intentions and plans.

Drafting

Drafts are rough plans or outlines that provide the skeleton for a book or article. It is the next stage on from planning and organizing your material. Drafts can be changed, adapted, scrapped: a final draft may seem nothing like the first one but this is evidence that the writer is continually thinking and adapting his or her ideas and words.

The way to do it is to jot down ideas, even words in any sequence, and think about, amend and alter the words (and pictures if needed) until you are satisfied with the order.

Activity

Select any one of these topics, or you can choose a topic that appeals to you more. Jot down thoughts, ideas, words and build them up into a rough draft of, say, 200 words. At this stage you don't need to worry about spelling and grammar. Finally, write out a neat copy of the draft: this should be the basis for the final article.

Select from:

1 A family event
2 'It could only happen to me . . . '
3 An article for your favourite magazine.

That's my word

The word-list and phrases that occur to you should be jotted down immediately: they may not necessarily be used but words are often a spur to a second set of thoughts. When you've written the final draft, check for these aspects:

1 Will the finished article capture a **reader's interest**?
2 Use arrows to indicate the **sequence** of ideas that will run through the article.
3 Will each paragraph have a unity and a **clear theme**?
4 Are ideas/words/paragraphs in the **right order**?
5 Will it have bite and **impact**? (What words or events will indicate impact?)

Editing and re-writing

You may be very lucky indeed and be able to write material that is immediately perfect and which requires no further work on it. Lucky but unlikely. Most writers, both famous and beginners, have to re-work their material several times before it satisfies them and their editor or publisher. There are skills to be learned here, skills that can be taught on a writer's course or understood through the hard discipline of self-improvement at the kitchen table or on the word processor.

Among the skills that should be applied are these:

1   Write in a logical sequence either of events, or dialogue, or plot, so the reader isn't confused. (However confident and experienced, writers can abandon this plan and introduce varied time sequences or flash-backs.)

2   When the first draft is completed, sleep on it and then read it through. Ask a friend or a member of the family to read and comment on it.

3   Based on your second-thoughts and external comments, revise your first draft, sharpening it up perhaps by compression, perhaps by deletion of words or sentences, perhaps by changing the sequence of events, ideas, dialogue.

4   This is editing, your own editing. It may be necessary to re-edit yet again when the story, the novel, the play, the poem is finished. So a third or fourth reading is required.

The message in this section is that good writing means re-writing. It may seem laborious. It is, but it is the writer's craft. If you can visit a library that contains manuscripts of famous novelists and playwrights, you will see their pages marked by revisions, crossings-out, new paragraphs and insertions. So you will not be alone in practising these necessary skills.

Summary

In this unit we have discussed the need to plan and structure one's writing. In particular, you ought now to:

- plan every piece of writing before embarking on the full story or article
- construct text by sequencing paragraphs into a story that fulfills the AIDA guidelines
- know that good writing is likely to require several drafts, revisions, and re-writing
- draft an article or story before writing it in full.

Assignment 1

To be attempted after completing Units 1, 2 and 3.
Time guide: 3 hours

Personal writing

This assignment requires you to demonstrate that you have tackled these aspects:

1   Researching the topic to establish factual accuracy
2   Planning and organizing your material
3   Drafting it so that there is evidence of sequence, continuity and management.

You can choose any one of the topics suggested in the first three units. These could be a personal episode such as a family crisis, an amusing event, a holiday that went wrong.

Or you can assume that you have been asked to write an article for a magazine on a sporting, social, food, fashion, entertainment or other topic.

The Assignment asks you to carry out two tasks:

1   Prepare a draft.
2   Write the full story or article (think about 800 words as a maximum length).

You could ask a friend or a member of your family to read your work for Assignment 1 and comment on it, or it could be used as part of a creative writing course and be assessed by a tutor.

UNIT 4

BUILD YOUR SKILLS

Objectives

After working through this unit you should be able to:
- describe (without achieving total mastery of) some of the essential skills needed for writing
- employ opportunities in the use of some of these skills in the activities and the review activity within this unit and in subsequent ones.

'This is the sort of English up with which I will not put'

(A marginal comment on a government document made by Winston Churchill)

Writing isn't at all like flying an aeroplane. A pilot has to spend weeks, months or years training before being let loose at the controls of Concorde.

A writer can pick up a pen and start **now**. Of course, there's some training (otherwise why should you be taking this course?). And there are skills that can be learned — research, grammar, spelling, editing. But writing begins with imagination and creativity and so it is possible to start writing immediately and to learn as you proceed. As Dr Johnson pointed out, over 200 years ago, 'A man may write at any time, if he will set himself doggedly to it.' (For 'man' assume 'woman' too, although Samuel Johnson was a notorious misogynist).

Nevertheless, there are some **skills** that a writer eventually requires. What are they?

Activity

Make a list of the skills that you think are needed by a writer.

A skills list

For this activity there isn't a quick and simple answer. You might have included grammar in your list but a proper answer to the activity requires a full chapter. Some of the essential skills are described in this section.

Reading

Most writers are avid readers. They consume other people's texts — admiring them, criticizing, perhaps even contemplating a little disguised copying. It's important (one is tempted to say 'necessary') to read widely. Take a wide spectrum of writing including the classics (Jane Austen, Shakespeare, Thomas Hardy), twentieth-century writers (D. H. Lawrence, Scott Fitzgerald), contemporary writers, feature writers on newspapers and magazines. And don't ignore the skills of journalists and editors: *The Sun* may not be to everyone's taste as a daily newspaper but they can teach you a lot about how to write a headline and summarize a complex topic in half a dozen sentences. *The Sun* also teaches us another lesson — to amuse people. If you make people smile, they'll read you, especially if, like Spike Milligan, no one is safe from mockery:

> 'A man called Vincent Van Gogh
> Developed an ear-splitting cough.
> No sleep could he get
> And he wouldn't have yet
> Had he not lopped the other ear off.'

Research

We've mentioned research several times already. A writer generally needs some reference books on the desk — a dictionary, Roget's *Thesaurus* (Penguin edition), perhaps an encyclopaedia and whatever books are needed for the specialist topic that is being tackled. Access to a good library is essential, too.

Research isn't only reading. It can also involve talking to people, visiting places and taking photographs.

Vocabulary

People should constantly add to their vocabulary. A good dictionary is needed. And a thesaurus is necessary for alternative words. An inexperienced writer uses the same words or phrases time and again: repetition is boring.

Spelling

If you are uncertain about your spelling don't let it put you off writing. Better to start and make errors than never try. On the other hand, words are a writer's currency. If you are uncertain, use a dictionary. Among the best ones at a reasonable price are Oxford Concise, Cassell and Longman dictionaries We all have blind spots on some words and a good idea is to keep a notebook at your elbow to jot down words that give you trouble — accommodation, necessary, business, ascent, accent — and so on. (Here's a test — which one of these three words is incorrect: occurrence, conscientious, advantagious).

Syntax

Grammar, punctuation and sentence-construction cannot be ignored, either. If you are to be a writer you will be using nouns, pronouns, verbs, adverbs, adjectives, prepositions, elisions and so on. Since you will be using a variety of words, why not find out what forms of speech they are? You can do this by consulting a fairly basic English grammar book, referring back to it when you are puzzled.

However, the good news is that many famous writers have a shaky grasp of grammar. This doesn't deter them, but they will need the help of a professional editor. Our advice is that the more you know about grammar, the more skilful you should become in the use of words (just as the skill of a pilot improves with knowledge of the aeroplane's controls).

Therefore, make a start with your writing even if your grasp of grammar and punctuation aren't precise. But have at your elbow the reference books already mentioned as well as a copy of Fowler's *Modern English Usage* (Penguin edition) or the *Longman Guide to English Usage*.

Activity

We haven't yet finished with a writer's skills but to vary the approach, attempt this activity. Assume that you have been asked to write an article on a local environmental or local historical topic for a newsletter or magazine. Where would you go to find out the information you are going to need?

'Clean up local history'

For environmental topics, your research might take in:

1   The local Council office — minutes of committee meetings; official reports; talk to the Planning Officer.
2   Local interest groups — conservationists, independent amenity groups: check at the library which may also have plans and reports on display.
3   Government reports on public health, transport and environmental concerns for your area.
4   Any other contacts?

For local history, there could be:

1   A collection of local history books in the public library.
2   Ancient citizens for 'human interest' stories (and perhaps rare photographs).
3   Church, museum and school records.
4   Any other sources?

Taking notes

This exercise brings us to another skill needed by writers — note-taking. There are a number of ways of taking, keeping and storing notes.

Random jotting is one way of keeping a notebook but it is not a satisfactory method. Another method is to use a tape recorder. But most people use handwritten notes as a means of recording information and ideas. The main problem with note-taking is that it can get out of hand, with multiple notebooks and no clear route through them. Therefore, one idea is to have a separate page for each piece of research indicating these elements:

1   Date and time
2   Person seen and spoken to, plus job title
3   Information from the inquiry
4   References to sources (books, and magazines, with dates)
5   Cross-references to several sources of information on the same theme

6 Any additional points that you want to make personally which you might draw on in writing your full account later.

A notebook is one way of keeping records. Notes should be brief and succinct.

Another method is an A4 ringbinder where separate pages of notes can be slipped in and arranged in an order that suits you.

Finally, the notebook/ringbinder should have an index.

Your route map

Another method of organizing your notes is to draw up a route map. By this means you can link ideas and information. For example, suppose the topic of your writing is built around a village or town: this is at the centre of the map with researched items as branches, something like the figure below.

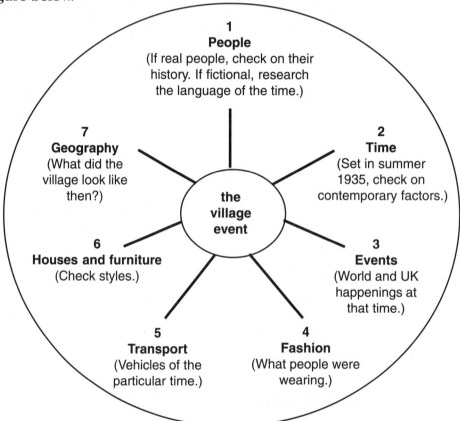

The advantage of this system is that it is elastic: a new topic or heading can be added to it and cross-referenced to the numbers in your notebook. For example, your notes might say

5 Transport: cars (Ford, Morris, Jowett, Armstrong-Siddeley, BSA motorcycle 350cc, etc.)

Using index cards

Another method used by professional writers is an index card system. Boxes of cards can be bought at a newsagent's shop, or you can make your own from paper. A different card is used for each topic. Each card is given a heading, perhaps in alphabetical order. Notes are added, for example on a technical topic:

7

> **Narrow boats**:
> English narrow boats were 70 feet x 7 feet, to fit within canal locks.
> Could carry up to 30 tons of cargo.
> Cabin aft.
> Lock key was heavy iron windlass to wind up.
> Sluices on lock-gates.
> Butty-boat was towed astern.

This method can be used with the route map, cross-referenced to numbers (top right).

These are some of the skills of note-taking. Like any other profession, writing needs organization, research and record-keeping.

Copyright

Before quoting or using other people's material, it is essential to check on copyright.

Activity

This activity sets you the task of researching copyright. You should use reference books such as the *Writers' and Artists' Yearbook*, an annual which is in every library.

The activity is to explain in your own words the copyright that attaches to an author's work, and also describe the publisher's rights. You will need to demonstrate some of the skills already suggested, namely :

1   Research
2   Note-taking
3   Summarizing quite complex information into readable and
      correct English.

Copyright counts

You might well have been disconcerted by the complexity of copyright. It extends not only to published writings, but also to film, video, drama, radio, television, music, computer software and so on.

The main rules to prevent copying which you should have isolated are these:

- copyright remains with the author during his or her lifetime and for 50 years after death
- authors (and other publishers) can quote from copyright material as long as the origin is acknowledged
- substantial quotations (the accepted rule is anything in excess of 400 words for a novel or a verse from a poem or song) requires the permission of the publisher acting for the author, and a fee may be payable

- a separate copyright exists in every published edition of a work—the publisher is entitled to this copyright for 25 years after the date of first publication.

These are the basic rules — you'd need a lawyer to untangle all the threads of copyright.

Style

Everyone has their own style of writing. In the formative stages of learning to be a writer, the style may be hesitant or naive. With practice a personal style of writing should emerge. It will be partly formed by the choice of words, phrasing, syntax. But beneath the words lies the author's voice, attitude and viewpoint. Not quite as Laurence Sterne put it (again, over 200 years ago): 'Writing . . . is but a different name for conversation.' Writing, unlike conversation, allows revision, a second (or third or more) chance. Eventually comes a writing style that reflects the character, personality, attitudes, opinions and thus the 'voice' of the creator. But, whatever style you adopt, it must be grammatically correct.

What, then, is 'good style'. Impossible to answer. You can recognize it in Jane Austen or Charlotte Bronte. Distinguished academics spend their careers analysing the style of classical writers so we aren't going to make much headway in a paragraph.

However, there are elements of 'good' style that can be listed for reflection and/or discussion.

- **Clarity**: a reader isn't amused or kept interested if the meaning isn't clear. (There are always exceptions, of course; the plays of Harold Pinter and Samuel Beckett are not entirely crystal clear in meaning.)
- **Economy**: an effective writer uses the correct (that is, appropriate) number of words or sentences to carry the meaning or the intention of the text. At its worst, economy can be incompleteness at one end of the scale, and prolixity and verbosity at the other extreme. Aim, therefore, for a style in between which is lucid and accurate.
- **Choice**: the choice of words to express emotions, actions or behaviour is one's own. But your choice indicates your feeling for words as well as your opinions or judgements. For example, some writers aim for a plain, unvarnished style, illustrated in their phraseology and phrasing. At the other extreme are writers who are ornamental. Others strive for power, or raciness, or wit, or severity.

You should seek a style that you are happy with because it will express your personality. At the same time, there are tricks of the trade: here are some of them.

Stylish tricks — and pitfalls

We learn by doing. Championship-winning golfers, whose swing seems so effortless, practise for at least three hours a day. Similarly, you could try to write at least a paragraph a day.

As you do, you'll find (and notice in newspapers and magazines) some tricks of the trade. Better to call them 'tools' rather than tricks. It sounds more professional. And, alongside the tricks are pitfalls.

Here are some of them.

Simile and metaphor

A simile compares different things by linking their common features, using as or like.

> His shoulders were as broad as those of King Kong with his brain matched in size. (P G Wodehouse)

A metaphor creates a picture-image by applying a name or phrase to an object. Examples are: 'a glaring error', 'food for thought' and so on. Over-used, they can be boring and weaken the pace of narrative.

Clichés

Footballers love them: 'at the end of the day'; 'a game of two halves'; 'sick as a parrot' (simile as well as a cliché). They are usually to be avoided because they demonstrate a writer's lack of vocabulary and imagination. However, there are occasions when a cliché could be used, perhaps mockingly to show you are aware of it deliberately and mockingly, as when one partner says of another (known for his or her miserliness), 'he's (or she's) generous to a fault'.

Tautology

This is saying the same thing twice over in different words. It's a stylistic fault and should be avoided at all costs. Examples are:

> *Immediately, as soon as she could . . .*

and

> *He went on to say, in his next sentence . . .*

Idiom

The English language is packed with them: idiom is peculiar phrasing accepted because of long use as in 'dressed to kill', 'fly in the ointment', 'daft as a brush'. They can be used to give colour to one's writing, but excessive use becomes boring.

Euphemism

This is saying something softly when the truth hurts. 'Dispensed with your services'; 'offered redundancy'; 'taking up a new challenge' are all alternatives to saying 'you've been sacked' (which is itself an idiom).

Syntax

Syntax is the grammatical structure of sentences, the links between words, phrases or clauses. Syntax is a daunting word for the clarity and logic of expression. If you aren't aware of it you could come up with sentences such as this one:

> *We all ran into the field, me, my Dad, the horse and Billy, our dog. He lay on his back and kicked his legs in the air.*

Yes, but out of the four possibilities, who is doing the kicking?

Really, it's very nice

When you complete any piece of writing and have it typed (or word-process it yourself), check it carefully for spelling, grammar and vocabulary. A second opinion is valuable. If you are sending anything for publication, the editor will correct mistakes. But before it gets this far, make sure the text is free from excessive wordiness. Pruning is painful but necessary. For example, cut out qualifying words — 'really', 'likely', 'very' — and delete unnecessary adjectives and adverbs. Superlatives are also suspect — 'longest', 'biggest', 'fattest', 'happiest'. In the first place, the words are too loose, too imprecise and secondly they can be challenged — you may think your hotel has 'the best view' but ten others will query your choice.

Review activity

This review activity, to be appropriate to this unit, could be devised as an exercise in grammatical construction. However, most potential authors hope that they left parsing and subordinate clauses behind them when they walked through the school gates for the last time.

Instead, to make the activity more interesting, first read these extracts from a newspaper article on a writers' conference and then tackle the task.

'With few exceptions, authors in the flesh are disappointingly like everyone else. Just like income tax inspectors they are decent, polite, ordinary, modest. And, sadly, some are a lot less interesting than tax inspectors. The reason? A writer's imaginative world comes alive when he or she, secluded in an attic, deep in the fastness of the night, puts pen to paper.'

'Yesterday, 40 or so aspirants sat at the feet of a best-selling author. No speech was offered: instead she offered to answer questions. These were given with extraordinary candour, sensitivity and wit. 'Just like St Joan' she said, mockingly, 'I really hear voices first'.

'How do you invent conversations?' asked one listener, daringly.

'By eavesdropping, by listening to people in buses, pubs, even walking behind them along a road — I'm not ashamed to take notes at café tables.'

And when?

'At home I write from near midnight to 4am when everyone else is in bed.'

'How do you find your themes?' someone else asked.

'Any page in a daily newspaper has six or more: love, betrayal, ambition, sex, money, death.'

'Some of the writers who attended the conference came from far afield: they differed in their choice and style of dress, accent and stories but they had one thing in common: they were determined that a worthwhile aim in life was to try to write a good book, an original book, and so to give expression to their individual voices.'

The task

Choose an event that you have been involved in. It could have been a conference, a meeting, a social event, a sports occasion. There are about 200 words in the short article on the writers' conference. Extending to 300 words or more, write an account 'in your own voice'. You should not strive formally for 'style' but you should aim to express a personal viewpoint, and since this is an exercise in a chapter on grammar, make sure that it is immaculately presented in terms of spelling, punctuation and grammar.

This review activity should not be sent to your tutor. However, it would be useful to obtain someone's verdict or opinion of it, so ask a friend or member of your family to read it.

Summary

In this unit, you have looked at:

- a skills list which all writers need to acquire — reading, research, some grammatical knowledge
- the importance of keeping accurate notes, planning thoroughly, and developing an individual style
- copyright and its implications
- some of the 'tricks of the trade' and the pitfalls associated with them.

UNIT 5

WRITING FOR MAGAZINES

Objectives

After working through this unit you should be able to:
- describe the major outlets for magazine writing
- appreciate some of the skills required to write effective articles
- through practice, write articles that are designed for a particular readership.

Magazines

It is estimated that around 10 000 magazines are published in the UK each year. They appear weekly, monthly, quarterly, even annually. If we multiply this figure by the number of editions, it means that a staggering total of around 300 000 editions require articles, news stories, competitions, short stories, crosswords, letters, photographs and other written and visual material. That's the UK; there are international magazines, too, which all adds up to a substantial market for published work.

In this unit we shall concentrate on non-fiction writing. This is itself a huge field with disparate markets.

Markets

Look at the magazine racks in a newsagent's shop. The range is wide but even so they display only a fraction of the total market available to journalists. Multiply the biggest W H Smith display of magazine titles by six and the total market comes into sight. Over 7000 periodicals that carry advertisements are listed in BRAD (see the end of this chapter). And there's over 2000 magazines that don't carry any advertising. All of them are looking for articles.

The discouraging aspect of this market analysis is that 90 per cent of articles are written by staff writers/journalists working full or part-time for the particular magazine. Which leaves ten per cent for freelance writers, some known, some unknown. Even so, opportunities are there and to raise your spirits, having depressed them, all magazine editors are looking for new writing talent or a different perspective on a familiar theme.

Selection

One way of grouping is to do it by readers. Publishers analyse their readership and reflect what they discover about readers in the content, style, price, covers, advertisements and their editorial slant.

Activity

To get you thinking about potential markets, make a subject classification based on the interests of potential readers, ranging from A to W. See if you can think of up to 30 subjects.

How did your answer compare with this list? There are 30 here. Did you think of other groups?

Animals	Fashion
Astronomy	Hobbies
Art	Homes and gardens
Antiques	International affairs
Books	Literary interests
Business and finance	Motoring and cars
Camping and climbing	Music
Children	Puzzles and crosswords
Computers	Sailing
County and regional interests	Sports
Current affairs	Teenage and pop
Education	Television and radio
Electronics	Transport
Engineering	Travel
Entertainment	Women's interests

Now, having made your list, select no more than three topics or subjects that you would regard as your specialist areas. What are they:

1 _____

2 _____

3 _____

Perfect circulation

Another way of regarding magazines is to look at their circulation figures. These are vitally important to publishing companies looking for advertising revenue and for copy sales. Sales are measured by ABC, the Audit Bureau of Circulation, which reports at six monthly intervals. Over a million copies of *Radio Times* and *TV Times* are sold weekly. Also high in the top fifty are *Woman's Weekly*, *Woman's Own*, *Woman's Realm*, *Woman* and *Woman and Home*, a statistic that tells you about the main target of consumer magazines. Women are special, there's no doubt, but they are particularly special as magazine-buyers: it is known that women buy over 85 per cent of all titles. The women's titles (above) are published by IPC Magazines; other major publishers are Condé-Nast (*House & Garden*, *Vogue*, etc.); EMAP (*Which Computer?*, *Mother & Baby*, etc.); Morgan-Grampian; Benn; Macmillan; The National Magazine Company; D C Thomson (*Beano* and *Dandy*); Argus House; HHL Publications and others.

Small is beautiful

These magazines and comics are the big sellers. However, there are thousands of specialist or regional magazines with small circulations. What they all have in common is a thirst for articles. The great majority of these are provided by journalists employed on the magazine or by known specialist freelance writers. The newcomer has to break into this magic circle and the way to do it is:

1 Find the right topic — research it; become confident in writing about it

and

2 Translate your knowledge into an article or text that is the right length, in the appropriate style and which matches the ages and interests of a selected magazine's readers.

All this assumes that writers of magazine articles hope to see their work published, and be paid a fee for it. But there are people who write 'shadow' articles and never post them. This unit is just as relevant to secret writers as it is for potential income-earners. So now let's explore some of these skills.

Research

Two kinds of research are required. One leads on from your interests or specialism — the topic (or topics) you've selected to write about. Some people can carry a lot of facts in their head; most of us cannot and so we need to research the topic, jotting down information, quotations and people's views in a notebook or pad.

The other kind of research is to find a suitable market for a potential article. Here are some guidelines to help with your search:

- Find out which magazines exist for readers who share your interests in a chosen topic.
- Read several different magazines on this topic.
- Study and analyse them for:
  — the **themes** of articles
  — the **length** of an average article
  — the **editorial objectives** and **writing style** (factual, descriptive, serious, amusing, domestic, adventurous).
- Is there a **common theme** in the articles (such as reviewing new equipment; personal stories; accounts of events).
- Having done all this, make your own short list (and keep adding to it) of your original ideas for new articles, fitting in with your analysis of the magazine's aims, content and style.
- Write a 'shadow' article as if for the magazine. You could get your tutor to read it, or send it to the magazine.

Structure and style

The next decision is on the type of article that is to be written. We begin, then, with purpose or objective. Is it to inform, to reflect on the past, to report on a visit or event, to instruct, to amuse — or what?

Your answer will depend on the research you do on the magazine and its readership. Editors generally want articles that fulfil at least two of these objectives — to report and amuse perhaps or inform and instruct.

Next, remember the reader and the communication spiral between writer and reader:

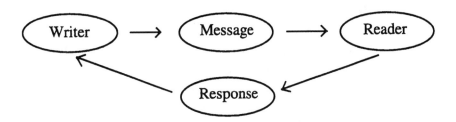

The master plan

Some people can sit down at their word processor and write. Good for them. For most of us, and as a sound piece of advice, make a plan. The resources are simple — a large sheet of paper and a pen (or a blank screen on the WP if you are electronically adept).

You begin the idea. This should be translated into the message — with an early decision taken on the purposes of the article (instruct, inform, amuse etc). Next, jot down paragraph numbers, say 1 to 6 or 8 for an 800-word article. Against the numbers write a word or two on the theme of each paragraph. This helps you to arrange your material in a logical sequence.

The next stage is to plot or summarize the information or points to be made in each paragraph. You could use a word or two for each idea or point, adding references to factual sources or quotations, if you intend to use them.

For example, suppose an article is being planned on a gardening topic. The structure could look like this:

Paragraph	Theme or topic	Ideas or points
1	Set the scene: it is autumn in the garden	Personal anecdote or gardener's tale
2	Problems at autumn time	Pruning, leaves, new planting: tips; facts
3	Pick on a famous garden (with pictures)	Interview with the gardener; best advice is .
4	Substantiate with more stories	Anecdotes
5	Select one or two plants/ flowers for special mention	Substantiate with facts and figures
6	What you can do . . .	Addresses etc

Activity

Choose a topic of your own. Follow the advice to decide on structure and sketch out the theme and ideas for each paragraph. Marshal your notes, cuttings from newspapers, items for research and random ideas in the right-hand column.

Style

Style is your own personal way of writing. If you make the mistake of copying someone else's style, you won't be happy with the result and it is likely to be false, anyway.

However, as you know from Unit 4, there are some basic rules of grammar and syntax. This isn't the place to describe the rights and wrongs of grammatical construction. There are plenty of grammar books available to help you.

Basically, however, you need to know the functions and variations that are applied to writing a paragraph, using sentence, phrases and clauses. A sentence must have a finite verb (a verb with a subject that it agrees with it in person and number). A phrase is a group of words without a finite verb. A clause is a sentence that acts as a link or qualification to another sentence.

Here's an example. Find a sentence, phrase and clause in this statement:

Please accept my resignation because I don't want to belong to any club that accepts me as a member.

(If you are interested, Groucho Marx wrote it.)

For an article, style is not only your writing style. Structure, content, paragraphing, sentence construction, the ordering of ideas — they are all vital elements of style. In short:

1 Content
2 Organization of ideas
3 Order and sequence
4 Grammatical construction, phrasing and sentences.

Comparing styles

Let us look at how two journalists demonstrate the techniques. Here are two brief introductions to articles on the same theme — health and fitness. Read them and compare their different styles.

'KEEPING IN TRIM

Exercise is good for you. There's no doubt about that, but for many people the very idea of donning a track suit and jogging around the park immediately sends them scuttling into the kitchen to consume a large cream bun for comfort.

There are methods of keeping in trim, however, and they need not be a form of torture, as many of us believe. There are many Keep Fit and Dance Studios whose main aim is to make it fun to take exercise.

The result of all exercise is that you should feel a lot better and a lot healthier after a short period. But if you overdo exercise, it can do you more harm than good, so it's a good idea to take advice from the experts who can help you to devise a scheme for your own level of personal fitness.

If you are shy about being seen in a leotard because you have some unsightly lumps in the wrong places, you can employ a personal fitness instructor who will come to your home. But for people who enjoy the social side of keeping in trim, there's a chance to make friends while becoming fit by joining a local health club or fitness centre.'

FIGHT THE FLAB!
"Mirror, mirror on the wall
 Do you like what you see when you bare all?"

'Do you know what is one of the biggest problems in the world today? It's having a BIG BUM. Some people can't avoid it, they've been born with a big one. But most of us can do something about it, as well as fighting his brother, BIG TUM.

There are two remedies. What are they?

1 Diet
2 Exercise

What about this for a statistic: over 60 per cent of people in the UK eat and drink more than 30 per cent more than they need. If you don't believe me, carry out the popular Eye Test on men in pubs: out of ten, how many are carrying a Heavy Load.

The first stop to keeping fit is watching and reducing your diet. But few people have strong enough willpower to discipline themselves in private. You need to join a slimming club. Weight loss isn't accompanied by voice loss, and so to fight the worry and the boredom of being a BMI 30 (3 stone or more overweight) you should join one of the clubs in your area: your local newspaper will be a big help in detecting them.

Secondly, exercise. You can do it by joining fitness classes, aerobics groups, dance schools or health centres. However, if you are a blushing rose and don't like to bounce the flab in public, a Personal Fitness Trainer can visit you at home to advise on diet and work-outs. The advantage of having your own tame PFT is that exercises can be tailored for you; you can choose your own music or generate your own groans and collapse without witnesses.'

Activity

Having read the two articles, spend ten minutes jotting down the differences between them.

What did you come up with?

The content is much the same. So too are the ideas which suggest that diet and exercise can be achieved in various ways. Order and sequence varies but it is in the style of writing that the major differences lie. 'Keeping in Trim' is straightforward, plain, unvarnished writing. It's also bland and a trifle dull. Also faintly apologetic, as if exercise is something we should all do, as if we'd rather prefer to be eating cream buns, avoiding physical torture and wearing something smarter than a leotard.

'Fight the Flab!' is ruder, gutsier, more direct — and more immediately readable. Instead of being all in one style and neatly balanced, it attempts dramatic verbal shock-tactics as in 'Mirror, mirror', 'Big Bum', 'BMI 30' and so on. Sentences are shorter and are skilfully sequenced (that is with one sentence or phrase encouraging you to read the next one).

You may prefer 'Keeping in Trim': we are not advocating one style in preference to another, only noting the differences.

Opening and closing

A positive and punchy opening is the key that opens the door to an editor's heart. The opening words — perhaps only ten of them — dictate whether or not the reader will move on. You must seize the attention of an editor — and thus all readers — in the first sentence.

A confident, lively opening is crucial. It sets the tone of the whole piece and if cleverly done, it will provide an insight into how you intend to write the remainder of the article. It answers a reader's first question: 'What's this all about?'

If you look at newspapers, you'll see one technique is a smart headline. Then comes the first sentence or phrase. Among the techniques used in the 'lead' are these:

- an applied quotation from a famous person or someone in the news — 'On your bike', perhaps, for a country holiday
- an anecdote — personal to you or from a famous person
- a shocking revelation that you've discovered — 'Wigan has the dirtiest beaches in Europe'
- ask a question — 'What's the best meal you've eaten — and the *worst*?'

It is all very well to have a good start, but the second sentence or paragraph has to maintain the pace and style. A long, rambling paragraph is dead wood. Once into the article, the argument or description should be developed, keeping the major points in logical order. 'Dead wood' occurs when too many adjectives crowd the verbs, or when descriptions or dialogue lose their point and impact in a flood of words. Aim to be succinct, not discursive (long-winded). Key sentences should capture the important points. And avoid the tempting 'I'. This pronoun is the refuge of the pompous and the egotist. There are other ways of adding individuality to your writing by avoiding 'I . . . . .' These are the methods of avoiding dead wood.

Short and long

A question often asked on creative writing courses is 'What's the best length for a paragraph?', or its companion 'How many words should there be in a sentence?' The answer to both questions is 'Don't know'. It all depends, and the dependence is based on the kind of magazine you have in mind, the subject, and your style. *The Sun* newspaper at one extreme likes sentences of no more than five words, less if possible and the newspaper has over 4.1 million daily sales. Other newspapers and magazines (the ones you read) may be more dignified and allow the writer to be more discursive. But the best advice is to err on the side of brevity for sentence-length and therefore five or six sentences per paragraph is as good a guide as any.

Closing

The close is as important as the opening. Don't drag out the farewell. A sharp, tight finale can be very effective, with the reader feeling that he or she is better informed or has been amused.

Activity

Again, look through some magazines and newspapers. Search for examples of effective openings and closings, and try to spot some stylistic tools (tricks of the trade) used in them. Jot down some examples.

A model

Let's look at a real example. This is part of an 800-word article in a women's magazine. The title is 'Travel for the Lazy'. Read the article and analyse it for the skills that have been described. To help you with your analysis, use the questions that follow the article.

TRAVEL FOR THE LAZY

'There's nothing like travel to make you lazy. Any excuse and I'll leap on a plane. Even at the check-in desk, I'm nodding off.

On the other hand, it seems to me that airline staff sometimes deliberately try to upset their customers. Do you wonder what they're saying to each other?

"Do you see those two? They've been giving each other the eye all the time they've been in the queue. Shall we do the decent thing and set them next to each other or shall we be really horrible and, at the last minute, say there's been a mix-up and shove him at the back? Serve him right — he's far too smarty-pants and self-assured for his own good. As for her? I know — K6 — the seat with the upward draught and the wonky back . . . Enjoy your flight, sir!"

As for me, because once on board the plane I'm totally relaxed, I willingly abdicate all responsibility and do everything I'm told when I'm told. But before boarding and abandoning all decision-making there is one last desperate moment of confusion at the check-in desk as I wonder which seat to ask for. Do I demand a window seat for the view or do I choose the aisle for easy access to the lavatory? One thing's for sure in this particular version of computer dating is that I don't want to be sitting next to some talkative, bouncy, unaccompanied minor all the way to Melbourne. Unaccompanied by all means, but over 18 if you please.

There are people who have strong ideas about how to handle flying. They drink only water, eat only fruit, put tea bags on their eyes and wrap their feet in iced towels. Me, I drink and eat everything that comes my way. I put my feet up, crash out and watch movies. If I've travelled thousands of miles and paid for the pleasure I want my body to know about it and remind me for days.

Long-distance flights are the best. I look upon them as blissful, uninterrupted hours when I can let my thoughts wander. Travel, for the most part, is about escaping. It's about time to reflect and put everything in perspective. It's about getting away from rules, regulations and mass opinion and our own opinion of ourselves as we battle with the elements of modern life. I know my escape route only too well. I don't take a slow slide into sloth. I go for the direct dive.

I'm never homesick and I love staying in hotels — all that people-watching while I lounge in busy lobbies and restaurants . . . I'm quite shameless. I don't just watch: I stare and eavesdrop as I try to work out who's doing what and to whom.

As I doze and dream, thoughts about the next meal begin to dominate my mind, especially in the hotel. Much as I enjoy perching on a bar stool, listening to stories as my cocktail is mixed, it's room service that appeals to me most. There's nothing like a late breakfast in bed and a club sandwich — with extra mayonnaise — in the afternoon to see you through until dinner.

Another luxury of being away are the hours you can fill having your legs waxed, your nails manicured, your hair done and your feet cossetted. I hate my feet. If I'd been born in China they could have been bound from infancy. As it is, I spend hours staring down at them, seeing them stretch out before me, my painted toenails almost lost in the distance. They might be slim but they're very, very long. Slim and long looks good on one's body. On the feet it looks ridiculous. It also makes buying shoes impossible. Through diet, exercise, a bit of surgical intervention and the attention of a good hairdresser, I've managed to work on every other bit of my body but there's absolutely nothing I can do about my ghastly feet. Well, I suppose I could take a holiday in China. The thing is, do they serve club sandwiches?'

Structure, content, style

Judge the article by using these questions.

1 Purpose: what is it — to instruct, inform, persuade, amuse? Is the article successful in meeting its objectives?

2 Idea and content: is the idea original in that it contradicts most people's perception that air travel creates anxiety? Instead, the writer tries to persuade us that, in her case, it is relaxing. Does the idea work?

3 Order and sequence: is the paragraphing effective in that one paragraph's theme leads into the next one?

4 Opening and closing: is the opening effective? (The contraction in the first sentence makes a vigorous lead.) And the closure — notice how the writer returns to food (mentioned earlier) in the last sentence.

5 Style: what do you think of it? Is the repetition of 'I' (which you've been warned against) effective, or not? As this is a personal statement, does she get away with it? Did you spot any clichés, tautologies and confused syntax?

6 Finally, did it work? The answer to the first question is that it is intended to be amusing and to offer a personal view of travel. If you were amused and read the article with interest to the end, it worked. What's your opinion?

Market guides

There are several useful books but these are pre-eminent:

BRAD (*British Rate and Data*). This monthly advertising guide is expensive so use the local library: it lists more than 7000 periodicals that carry advertising material. From BRAD, Maclean Hunter Ltd, Chalk Lane, Cockfosters Road, Barnet, Herts EN4 0BU.

Benn's Media Directory lists over 15 000 UK organizations. From Benn Business Information Services Ltd, PO Box 20, Sovereign Way, Tonbridge, Kent TN9 1RQ.

Willing's Press Guide is an alphabetical list of over 1000 periodicals. From Reed Information Services, Windsor Court, East Grinstead House, East Grinstead, West Sussex RH19 1XA.

Magazine News and the *Magazine Handbook* are published by the Periodical Publishers Association (PPA) which represents over 200 publishing companies that are responsible for about 1500 titles. PPA, 15 Kingsway, London WC2B 6UN.

Summary

This unit has just touched the surface of writing for periodicals, magazines and journals. You should now be better informed, and having tackled the Activities and the linked Assignment, you should be more expert.

However, there's a lot more to this subject than can be covered in a unit, and if you hope to become a successful freelance journalist, you should read an excellent guidebook, *Writing for Magazines* by Jill Dick, published by A & C Black.

Assignment 2

To be attempted after completing Unit 5.
Time guide: 4 hours

Magazine article

The objective is to write an article as if for publication by a magazine. These are the guidelines:

1 First, choose a topic or idea. This can be your own choice. For example, it could be on the home, gardening, holidays, antiques, sport, a leisure interest, health, food, wine — choose a topic.

2 Next, research it. Use the guidelines to decide on content, sequence and style, investigating facts and making notes on a grid.

3 Decide on your market, your readership. Pick out three magazines that you know or that you have researched that could be possible targets for the article.

4 Decide on length. We would suggest an article of between 600 and 1000 words.

5 Write it, following the advice on structure, sequence, grammar, spelling, vocabulary, phrasing.

6 Having written it, ask a friend or friends to read it, giving their opinion. Revise it in the light of comments.

When completed, and you are satisfied with it, you could ask someone in your family or a friend to read Assignment 2 and comment on it, or use it as part of a creative writing course.

UNIT 6

SHORT STORIES

Objectives

This unit describes the different elements in short stories, helps to identify sources and provides some ideas on how to structure a short story.

When you have completed this unit you should be able to

- identify potential sources for short stories
- appreciate the skills and components necessary for the construction of a well-crafted short story
- recognize the range of ingredients in a short story such as dialogue, character, description and conclusion
- draft an outline for a short story
- write a short story, ensuring that some of the different elements are included in it.

The short story — ancient and modern

The short story has a long history. It probably originated in oral tales told by an older generation to a younger one. Recorded (that is published) short stories are in the literary heritage of every language. In the English language and coming closer to our own time, among distinguished short story writers are (to name but six from what could be a lengthy list) Charles Dickens, Thomas Hardy, D. H. Lawrence, Saki (H. H. Munro), Dorothy Parker and John Updike.

Activity

Consider for a moment the reasons why short stories are probably the most popular form of creative writing. One shriekingly obvious answer is 'shortness'. But there are other reasons: jot down in your notebook what you think they are.

Short — but beautifully formed

Among possible answers are these:

- **Short** — but how short is a short story? At its briefest, let's say 400 words: two or three paragraphs only. Not much room for excitement and tension here. At its longest, 10 000 words could be the maximum. In between, anything goes. That's the definition of shortness.
- It's **easier** than writing a long story. Stating the obvious is a pitfall to avoid: we've just done it. But let's examine the 'easiness'. A short story could have all the elements of a novel — plot, character, atmosphere, conflict and action; beginning, middle and end; and

a final stimulating conclusion. One therefore begins to qualify on 'easier'. However, let it go.

- It concentrates on a **single theme or idea**. Generally true. Because space is limited, a short story may have a single idea, theme or concept which is swiftly worked out.
- **Succinctness** is a virtue. A short story forces the writer to crystallize an idea, develop it into a story, and tell it without too much embroidery. Many readers (especially public library borrowers) like short stories because they can be read in a single sitting, can be grasped (or enjoyed) swiftly, and can be savoured as a complete experience rather like drinking a glass of good wine.
- Short story writing can be viewed as a kind of **apprenticeship** that could lead to more ambitious projects such as a novel.
- They can be viewed a **short novels**. This means they have much the same structure of a novel but are simply shorter. William Trevor, a brilliant exponent of the genre, described a Chekhov story as 'the art of the glimpse'.

Markets

These are all positive points. On the other hand the market for the sale of short stories isn't large. Some national magazines feature stories, and some book publishers will look at a collection. More positively, the market for short stories is varied with many local magazines willing to consider stories from local writers who they can feature in the magazine or newspaper. And another thing in one's favour is that these outlets (national and local magazines and specialist publishers) encourage and look for good examples of creative writing, as distinct from factual reporting.

Sources

Where do you find the inspiration for a short story? Again, let's turn this question into an active search.

Activity

Write down your list of possible sources for short stories. They could be your own inspiration or assumed from reading stories by professional (and amateur) writers.

Inspiration or perspiration

Some ideas might leap at you. Others can emerge from thought, conversation, argument or by overhearing a remark in the bus queue. In your list might be:

- a personal experience (remember Virginia Woolf's comment about Jane Austen's stories, which she said were based on 'I love, I hate, I suffer')
- someone else's personal experience, told to you or overheard
- a picture or a photograph

- a newspaper or magazine story
- from personal observation of an unusual event or incident
- a holiday happening
- an idea thrown up by your reading of a novel or a story which you can change by altering the characters, the plot or the ending
- from a musical, theatrical, sporting or social event
- by concentrating on a person — real or imagined — and building a story around him or her.

Any other ideas?

For example here are three items plucked from the pages of local and national newspapers. Spend ten minutes on each one, thinking about a short story that could emerge from each news story.

1   Holiday nightmare

This year, the Burton family didn't enjoy their holiday. They had booked two weeks in a French *gite*, deep in the Provence countryside. After a long and tiring car journey, Mum, Dad and three junior Burtons arrived at journey's end. But where was it? Not a sign. Maps were consulted. Yes, they were at the right place. At the end of this track, there should be a stone *gite*, wood fire blazing, bowls of *potage* on the table. Instead, nothing.

Three hours and a lot of 'Pardon, monsieurs' later, they were in a local hotel. There was an explanation, but by the time they heard it, the Burtons' English sangfroid was in tatters.

2   Sale or return

Rose Whitcomb advertised in her local newspaper: 'For sale: compass made of wood and brass, with the maker's name Rich. Glynne. Offers.'

The offers didn't stop. First of all came three different local collectors who quickly raised their first offers of £20 to £200. But then some dealers heard about it. In the 18th century, Richard Glynne had made compasses for long sea journeys and it transpired that Rose's heirloom, given to her by her grandfather, was very rare indeed. £200 became £2000, then £10 000. Rose popped her pension book in her bag and set off for Sotheby's.

3   Wildcat in Essex

The third reported sighting of a wildcat came yesterday from Essex. Unlikely? Could be. If there are any wildcats in Britain, their habitat must be in the Scottish Highlands, not in Dagenham. But Jimmy Jackson swears he saw one, and he'd only had one drink at the Whip and Collar. That's the third report of the Essex Mog. What about the rest of Britain. Do you have a wild animal living near you? (Outside, that is, not indoors.) If so, let us know.

Keep a record

If you are stumped for ideas for short stories, keep a folder. Cut out news items such as these, and store them. They can provide a rich source for ideas, plots and sub-plots.

Planning

A short story, just like a novel, needs to be carefully planned. There is a longer explanation of plot construction in a later unit in this book, on novel-writing. You should read it alongside this unit on short stories because the discipline is the same.

Any story, short or long, needs a beginning, a middle (with the story development) and an end. You could write short stories without a structure such as this but it would be difficult to find a publisher for them. You could, for instance, write a story that concentrates on atmosphere rather than plot, or be a conversation between two or more people, or be a series of episodes without a clear link. All these varieties are possible: they can be practised and kept in your private folder.

Activity

Now plan out a story on a subject or theme that interests you. Think of start, middle, end. First, jot down in your notebook the ideas that would be contained in these three sections.

	Points to note
Start:	First paragraph needs to be sharp and short, an invitation to read on.
Middle:	No padding. Everything said in dialogue or in description must be relevant.
End:	Must be decisive, bold. Could have a final unexpected twist.

Plot and character development

A novel, being a longer story, generally requires these elements: theme; plot; characters; action; conflict; relationships between characters developed into sub-plots; conclusion.

A short story needs some of these, if not all. For example, there generally isn't room for sub-plots, character-development or character-interchange. There tends to be a single theme, worked out in very few characters, based on a single plot.

Activity

Having divided a story into its three parts, now write down numbers, from 1 to 10 or more. Against each number, write a line or two to indicate character introduction or plot development. This exercise ensures logical sequencing of the ideas that make up the story. Set it out like this:

		Points to note
Start	1	Sharp introduction
	2	
Middle	3	First hint of plot
	4	Character, plot, action, conflict, atmosphere are all developed
	5	
	6	
	7	
	8	
End	9	Climax with possible story twist
	10	

Making a start

If we look at some examples, it is possible to see how professional writers have dealt with these considerations.

LADY BARBARA AND SON

This story was written 60 years ago by Saki (H. H. Munro). His sparkling wit has survived the passage of years. The first few lines immediately establish the parameters of a unique, biting style.

'It was distinctly hard lines for Lady Barbara, who came of good fighting stock, and was one of the bravest women of her generation, that her son should be so undisguisedly a coward. Whatever good qualities Lester Slaggby may have possessed, and he was in some respects charming, courage could certainly never be imputed to him. As a child he had suffered from childish timidity, as a boy from unboyish funk, and as a youth he had exchanged unreasoning fears for others which were more formidable from the fact of having a carefully-thought-out basis. He was frankly afraid of animals, nervous with firearms, and never crossed the Channel without mentally comparing the numerical proportion of life belts to passengers. On horseback he seemed to require as many hands as a Hindu god, at least four for clutching the reins, and two more for patting the horse soothingly on the neck. Lady Barbara no longer pretended not to see her son's prevailing weakness; with her usual courage she faced the knowledge of it squarely, and, mother-like, loved him none the less.'

'LISTENING TO THE SILENCE'

Muriel Spark, author of radio plays, poems, short stories and novels (including *The Prime of Miss Jean Brodie*) is a modern writer. Her wit is also sharp and clean, just like Saki's, with comical and entertaining characters that spring to life.

Compare this opening from a Muriel Spark story.

'So great was the noise during the day that I used to lie awake at night listening to the silence. Eventually, I fell asleep contented, filled with soundlessness, but while I was awake I enjoyed the experience of darkness, thought, memory, sweet anticipations. I heard the silence. It was in those days of the early 'fifties of this century that I formed the habit of insomnia. Insomnia is not bad in itself. You can lie awake at night and think; the quality of insomnia depends entirely on what you decide to think of. Can you decide to think? — Yes, you can. You can put your mind to anything most of the time. You can sit peacefully in front of a blank television set, just watching nothing; and sooner or later you can make you own programme much better than the mass product. It's fun, you should try it. You can put anyone you like on the screen, alone or in company, saying and doing what you want them to do, with yourself in the middle if you prefer it that way.'

©Muriel Spark, 1988

Compare notes

In a few lines Lester Slaggby comes to life: note the nouns and adjectives which add up to a substantial indictment — 'charming', 'coward', 'timidity', 'funk'. Phrases are even more damning — 'frankly afraid of animals', and longer asides crush his character beyond repair — 'never crossed the Channel without mentally comparing the numerical proportion of life belts to passengers'. Furthermore, two sentences about Lady Barbara give us the clues to her personality.

Muriel Spark's opening paragraph builds a character, too, but it is through the first person and it also introduces a general condition — insomnia. It immediately engages the interest of the reader by asking you to compare your insomnia with the narrator's. Notice, too, the style: the mixture of short and long sentences, a question put and answered; the collection of images aroused by being awake in the dark — 'darkness, thought, memory, sweet anticipations'.

Activity

These two extracts are the start of stories. They are both written in descriptive language. Other starting-points for short stories come in dialogue. Whatever form they take, do they pass the test of tempting you to read on?

For each story there's also a middle and end. On a visit to the library, look through some collections of short stories to find some examples of effective endings.

Further study

There are collections of the best short stories both from the past and from contemporary writing that should be dipped into if you hope to extend your skills. For instance, there are collections of stories by some of the 'greats' such as Aldous Huxley, D H Lawrence, Guy de Maupassant, Somerset Maugham, Jean Rhys, Dorothy Parker, Katherine Mansfield, Edna O'Brien and many others. Or there are collections by different modern authors, such as *The Best Short Stories 1994* (and previous years, published by Heinemann), or *Modern Short Stories*, Faber.

Review activity

Choose a particular category: crime, romance, family, horror or any other genre. Try your hand at writing a short story, let's say between 1000 and 2500 words. You could give this assignment to your tutor to read, or try it out on family or friends.

Summary

In this unit you have been introduced to the main aspects of writing short stories. Sources, structure and writing styles have a great deal in common with novel-writing, and these skills are explained in more detail in Unit 11 on the novel.

You should here have considered and written pieces to indicate your thoughts on

- sources of stories
- structure
- comparison of styles.

UNIT 7

WRITING FOR CHILDREN

Objectives

When you have completed this unit you should be able to:
- distinguish the different audiences for children's writing
- identify different objectives for fictional and non-fictional writing and for poetry for children
- appreciate the writing skills demonstrated by published authors
- make an attempt at writing for children in one or more formats for different age groups.

It's not at all easy

At the offices of one famous publisher of children's stories a weary editor was heard to remark 'There's that lorry again. It must be the Tuesday delivery of Mums' stories.'

There's some truth in the cynicism. Every Mum reads stories to her kids. (Well, alright, almost every Mum). Every Mum has her own story. Therefore, Mum thinks, 'I'll write this down and send it to a publisher.' And Dads tell and write stories, too, adding to the lorry load.

Exaggeration? Patronizing and insulting to Mums (and Dads)?

Yes, all that.

But there's some truth in it. Writing for children seems easy because the language is simple, stories are uncluttered and there's not the problem of what is to happen in chapter 22 or page 359. As a result, writers of children's books are not as highly regarded as writers of adult books. They are thought of by many people as beginners, in the way that their audience are also in the early stages of learning.

There are three consequences from this line of thought:

1 Many beginner-writers start with a children's book because they think it's easy

and

2 the quality of the writing suffers because would-be authors think all they have to do is to put into written words a story told to a child at bed-time

and

3 there's a flood of material sent to publishers of material that is inadequate in thought, language and storyline.

True skills

Writing for children requires all the writing skills. If anything it's **more** difficult because the author has to imagine how a child views and thinks about the way that people behave. Perhaps the best advice to a beginner is to read or re-read some authors who are skilled writers and who have brilliantly demonstrated that they can see things with a child's eye. Among such a distinguished list would be Lewis Carroll, Arthur Ransome, Roald Dahl, Enid Blyton, Richmal Crompton, Beatrix Potter— and many others.

Activity

Before we are swept away by any more distracting generalizations, let's put down your own views. What, in your opinion, are the best qualities (the **essential** qualities) of the best writing for children?

Dahl's way

Perhaps the best way to answer this activity is to give an example of an outstanding children's author and analyse its qualities.

This extract is from *Charlie and the Chocolate Factory* by Roald Dahl. Charlie Bucket finds the fifth Willy Wonka prize ticket, allowing a select group of children ('just five, mind you, and no more') to visit and tour Willy's factory and have 'enough chocolates and sweets to last them for the rest of their lives!'

Some prize, some story.

Here is the extract:

'Charlie burst through the front door, shouting, '*Mother*! *Mother*! *Mother*!'

Mrs Bucket was in the old grandparents' room, serving them their evening soup.

'*Mother*!' yelled Charlie, rushing in on them like a hurricane. 'Look! I've got it! Look, Mother, look! The last Golden Ticket! It's mine! I found some money in the street and I bought two bars of chocolate and the second one had the Golden Ticket and there were crowds of people all around me wanting to see it and the shopkeeper rescued me and I ran all the way home and here I am! IT'S THE FIFTH GOLDEN TICKET, MOTHER, AND I'VE FOUND IT!'

Mrs Bucket simply stood and stared, while the four old grandparents, who were sitting up in bed balancing bowls of soup on their laps, all dropped their spoons with a clatter and froze against their pillows.

For about ten seconds there was absolute silence in the room. Nobody dared to speak or move. It was a magic moment.

Then very softly, Grandpa Joe said, 'You're pulling our legs. Charlie, aren't you. You're having a little joke?'

'I am *not*!' cried Charlie, rushing up to the bed and holding out the large and beautiful Golden Ticket for him to see.

Grandpa Joe leaned forward and took a close look, his nose almost touching the ticket. The others watched him, waiting for the verdict.

Then very slowly, with a slow and marvellous grin spreading all over his face, Grandpa Joe lifted his head and looked straight at Charlie. The colour was rushing to his cheeks, and his eyes were wide open, shining with joy, and in the centre of each eye, right in the very centre, in the black pupil, a little spark of wild excitement was slowly dancing. Then the old man took a deep breath, and suddenly, with no warning whatsoever, an explosion seemed to take place inside him. He threw up his arms and yelled '*Yippeeeeee*' And at the same time, his long bony body rose up out of the bed and his bowl of soup went flying into the face of Grandma Josephine, and in one fantastic leap, this old fellow of ninety-six and a half, who hadn't been out of bed these last twenty years, jumped on to the floor and started doing a dance of victory in his pyjamas.'

What's so special about Charlie's win?

Some of the qualities of Roald Dahl's writing can be picked out.

1 The readership is said to be 'under-nines'. Dahl speaks directly to them. There's no 'talking-down' by a grown-up to a youngster, no need for interpretation by an adult. Dahl goes straight to his readers.

2 The story has pace and bite. The first line is crucial in children's writing to capture the distinctive voice of the author and to capture immediate interest. Charlie bursts in with his news. The family is stunned until Grandpa Joe causes mayhem. All in two pages.

3 It's funny. Grandpa Joe, 96 and a half, throws his soup in Grandma's face and does a dance of victory. Children love to be amused: Dahl's zany stories give them many opportunities to laugh.

4 It's magical. Not apparent here, but the story is of how poor little Charlie, who has one bar of chocolate a year, becomes the protegé of a chocolate factory owner dressed in 'bottle green trousers, a back top hat on his head, a tailcoat of plum-coloured velvet and carrying a gold-tipped walking cane.'

5 Construction and language: the usual advice given to children's writers is to use short sentences, paragraphs and chapters. Dahl broke these rules, too, as he did with many others. In this extract, notice that the first two paragraphs are a line only each but the last paragraph is substantially longer.

The language is suitable for under 9's but Dahl was never afraid to use challenging words if they were appropriate.

6 Dialogue: Dahl's characters don't waste time or words — notice here too the use of italics, capitals and exclamation marks to emphasize dramatic speech.

7 Style: Dahl's stories were (and still are) tremendously popular with children because of the vigour of his imagination. Amazing, daft stories told with great humour and energy, and featuring children as heroes. An irresistible combination of story, characterization and skilful writing adds up to Dahl's unique style.

Activity

Using the Roald Dahl extract as a guide, let us return now to the original question which was to decide on the qualities that mark out the best kind of writing for children. Another way of approaching this elusive target is to make up a chart of the do's and don'ts of children's writing.

> Complete this chart, distinguishing between three age groups.
> A couple of entries have been put in to get you started.

	Children's age group	Do's	Don'ts
1	Two to seven	Pictures are essential	
2	Seven to twelve		Don't go in for lengthy descriptions
3	Older children of twelve plus	Use personal problems and conflicts to maintain the story's pace	

Writing for different age-groups

The three age-groups that are generally used as convenient sub-divisions are three to six; six to twelve and the teenager market, that is twelve to about sixteen. By the time they are aged fifteen to sixteen (or in many cases younger) teenagers prefer to read adult novels, that is when they can been diverted from teenage and adult magazines, quiz books, colour supplements and music magazines.

There are no inexorable 'rules' for each of these age-groups but there is plenty of room for common-sense. If you are keen to write for your own or friends' children, without any expectation of being published, you are bound by very few disciplines. However, if your ambition is to be published, you need to be aware of publishers' expectations.

Age two to seven

The best preparation is to go into a bookshop and look at the shelves or display stands. They are dominated by picture books. Children of this age who are being read to or who are learning to read for themselves need pictures to stimulate them and to hold their interest through a very short story.

The categories in this age group are picture books (including 'board' books) for two to seven year-olds, (i.e. books to be looked at by an adult and child together) and story books for beginner-readers (four to seven years of age).

Children's book illustrators are a small and highly talented group. Look particularly at picture books written and illustrated by Janet and Allan Ahlberg, Raymond Briggs, Michael Foreman, Colin McNaughton, Jill Murphy or Jan Pienkowski. These are professionals who have immense talent and who make their living from this specialized work. It is unlikely that you will be able to break into the select band of illustrators. You may, of course, have an undiscovered artistic talent and no door is ever fully closed so if your illustrations have merit, it would be worthwhile to send them to an agent or a publisher for comment.

Alternatively, you could write stories and suggest that the publisher finds an illustrator. The competition is severe both in terms of the volume of writers and the range of talent, but to be positive, you could select your best work and send it to a publisher. Before doing so you'd be wise to have your work read by a tutor, another children's writer or by colleagues and friends, in order to gain access to constructive criticism.

Basic rules, two to seven

Picture books

Children at this age love a story. Picture books are designed to keep the story moving. If you look closely at picture books you will see that they are generally sixteen or thirty-two pages with each double-spread of two facing pages carrying an episode in the story. Skilful writers and illustrators use one spread to lead the reader to the next ('and what do you think happened next?'). Another 'rule' is that text shouldn't duplicate the pictures but add to it. Look at a Raymond Briggs' Father Christmas or Fungus books to see how it is done.

You'll find some picture book authors write the text and draw/paint the pictures. But not always. If you are seeking publication, a publisher will, however, look to see if you understand the construction of a picture book and therefore the presentation of the text in double-page spreads helps a lot. Look at some famous picture-stories — Raymond Briggs, Maurice Sendak (*Where the Wild Things Are*), Helen Cresswell (Meg and Mog books), the Ahlbergs (*Each Peach Pear Plum*), and so on.

Telling the story

For the older end of this age group, and into the next one, the story is the key. A 'good' story (for any age) should have a brisk beginning, middle sequences that keep the pot boiling, and a lively, perhaps unusual, finish. Children like to be surprised, which suggests you might avoid an obvious ending. Most like animals (Paddington the Bear) that can take on all the characteristics of humans and a few animal extra ones.

Above all, a book needs an idea. This is the whole point of the book. For example, suppose you decide to write about a family — Mum, Dad, baby, big brother or sister, cat or dog.

Boring!

Unless.

The 'unless' is the point of the story; the 'view' taken by the author. Big brother/sister must have a vigorous personality — expressed in a few words or lines (or drawings). The cat/dog might act in a dastardly fashion. Perhaps magic, or fantasy, or bad behaviour comes into it. One of the cleverest titles is *My Naughty Little Sister* by Dorothy Edwards. Simple, but clever. The idea that your sister is naughty and you (aged four to eight), smugly innocent, can sit back and enjoy her antics, is very attractive.

Activity

Try it. Spend 20 minutes thinking ('thinking time' is just as important as 'writing time'). Think (and jot down) some characters for a story. Give them names (and don't be afraid to experiment: Violet Elizabeth Bott was a masterful invention for Just William's gang). Finally, what's your view. Put another way, what happens; what's the point of the story.

Age seven to twelve

If, out of the blue, you were asked to write about rabbits, or cricketers, or deep sea divers, what would you do? You'd study them, of course. Similarly with children. Your best apprenticeship for any age group is to observe them. Unobtrusively, if possible: watch them at play; mark (and make notes) of their conversation; listen carefully to their speech and watch how they respond to each other and to adults. This is a kind of apprenticeship and it can be immensely useful.

In your research you'll discover that for this age-group the appeal is in **stories**. But what kind of stories? There are no hard and fast rules, but stories in which children take part have been successful time and again. And the stories do not have to be part of the child's experience: among popular topics are cops and robbers, mysteries, space travel, school, family, fantasy, adventure, historical. The choice of field is limitless.

Stories can also be transferred. For example, Robert Westall read a newspaper item about how a gang of Dutch children found a wrecked Allied bomber, twenty-five years after the war had ended, dismantled the rear turret gun, transported it to a hideout and were just about the fire it when the police caught them. Westall transposed the story to Tyneside, placed it in the Second World War and had a group of children assemble and fire the gun.

Whatever the story, the elements of good writing are the same: story, individual storyline; believable characters, including children; a spice of danger and plenty of excitement; and speech that reflects the ways that children speak, not adults.

The twelve to sixteen-year age group

Instead of giving you the answers, think some out for yourself.

Activity

What factors have to be considered in stories for older children and teenagers?

Apart from the considerations already suggested, these points should feature in your reflections:

1 A story line or **plot** that these readers can identify with: contemporary social and family situations might seem relevant.

On the other hand many children enjoy stories remote from their own experiences, such as historical or science-fiction novels or stories set in other parts of the world. As proof, the historical novels of Joan Aiken and Rosemary Sutcliff, among others, provide continuing evidence.

2 **Characters** that are believable and interesting. Again, they might be contemporaries or from remote times or places but they must be 'real' and not cardboard stereotypes.

3 **Dialogue**: some stories are told entirely in dialogue; most mix dialogue with descriptive language. Word choice has to be closely controlled.

You are likely to have suggested other points. The danger of this kind of tendentiousness is to lay down rules and then think of authors who break every 'rule'. Guidelines on children's writing should therefore be regarded with some suspicion: an answer to the question 'What is good children's writing?' could be the same as that attributed to Louis Armstrong who when asked 'What is jazz?' replied, 'Man, if you gotta ask, you'll never know.'

Activity

Go to a library or to a bookshop and select any children's book, for any of the three age-groups. Read it and then in your own words explain why you think it is a winner.

This activity is not only a test of your critical judgement, but also an opportunity to write in your own developing style. You should reflect on these aspects:

- content, story, structure
- characterization
- vocabulary, syntax and style
- description and dialogue
- your final judgement.

Writing non-fiction

Stories aren't the only things children need. They are thirsty for information. So too are their teachers who set up project after project. This is another specialist field. The writer has to be expert in at least two ways:

- in the information area — history, science, geography
- in knowledge of children's learning.

The worst information books ignore or neglect the readers' needs. The best ones fulfil knowledge of subject and youngsters, but add a third — exceptional design, layout, illustration. To make sure mistakes aren't made, publishers ask the advice of educationalists — advisers, teachers, psychologists, and they choose designers with as much care.

As well as the other talents, writers of information books need lucidity. Every phrase and sentence should be considered, and shaped, to match the needs of the book's purpose, and be appropriate to the target age-group.

The books? They range from dictionaries and other word-books, atlases, encyclopaedias, poetry anthologies, songbooks, crafts, sports handbooks, and the biggest group of all — information books.

Activity

Suppose you were commissioned to write a children's non-fiction book (or books). Think about it.

- Which **topic** or topic-area is your choice?
- Which **age-group** would your book be aimed at?
- What is its **purpose** — information, a workbook with assignments, structured learning, or what?
- Estimate its **length** in words. Would there be illustrations, and if so, what kind — cartoons, drawn artwork, photographs, colour?
- **Style**: would it be factual only; any humour in it?

To take this activity further, draft or write a page of text for a non-fiction book.

Summary

In this unit you were introduced to some of the guidelines that govern writing for children. What you should have learned is:

- the importance of imagination and creativity in writing a story that has a distinctive view
- to think about how children react to your story, that is to construct story, characters and language from a child's level
- to realize that there are special skills in writing fiction or non-fiction for youngsters and these skills must be studied and practised.

Assignment 3

To be attempted after completing Unit 7.
Time guide: 3 hours

This assignment asks you to try your hand at writing a children's story or a non-fiction book.

(a) If your intention is to write a novel for children of, say, nine to sixteen, write an outline and a specimen chapter. You should specify the age-group, and give pen-pictures of the characters as well as provide details of the story line.

(b) Alternatively, write for a younger age group (say three to six or five to nine). In this case you should be able to write the story in full.

(c) Thirdly, you may wish to write a picture-story either with or without the pictures for the youngest age-group. You should write the story page by page, whether illustrating it yourself or else giving written instructions for an illustrator.

(d) Another alternative is to write for a group of children who are disabled in some way.

(e) Or write an outline with a few pages, of a non-fiction children's book of your choice.

Whichever alternative you choose, write (or type) the story as if preparing for publication.

You may wish to ask a member of your family, or a friend, or a tutor to read Assignment 3 and comment on it.

Going further

If you are interested in pursuing children's writing, improving your skills, and learning from the experts, you should read an excellent guidebook, *Writing for Children* by Margaret Clark, a publisher of children's books. For an older group, *How to Write for Teenagers* by David Silwyn Williams is also highly recommended.

UNIT 8

AUTOBIOGRAPHY AND BIOGRAPHY

Objectives

This unit describes the different forms of autobiography and biography; it requires you to undertake some reading in the genre; and it sets some tasks to explore and develop your skills. When you have completed this unit you should be better able to:

- identify the range of published and unpublished writing about people
- reflect on the skills needed to write effectively for a public or a private audience
- draw on personal experiences of yourself or others in order to practise some of the skills required for effective writing
- be aware of some of the dangers in this form of writing, such as the law of libel.

Autobiography

It is tempting to think that autobiography is one of the easier forms of writing. Why? Because you are writing about yourself and there's no one more expert than you on that particular subject. Oscar Wilde had a stylish aphorism to express it: 'I am the only person in the world I should like to know thoroughly'.

However, we should consider the word 'easy' more carefully. Most writers would say that it isn't at all easy, The mountain of publishers' rejection slips, matched by another Matterhorn of boring 'this is me' printed volumes, might indicate that there's a grain of truth in this observation. Furthermore, it is essential to avoid hurting other people who have featured in your life. An unkind opinion, put into writing, can have very damaging consequences both for families and friends, so it is essential to think of others before surrendering to absolute sincerity.

The dangers and weaknesses in writing about yourself might not appear too obvious so let's start by considering them. Before we go any further, reflect on the pitfalls.

Activity

What are the weaknesses that you have detected or which now occur to you in writing or reading autobiographies?

'Other people are quite dreadful'

Your answer might include some of these:

1 Egotism: autobiography can be the first refuge for conceit.
2 Bias: there is the temptation, often not resisted, to view other people's opinions as inferior to one's own.
3 Audience-neglect: unless the person is exceptionally brilliant or has led an exciting life, a single viewpoint on personal or world events can be a boring experience for the reader.
4 Pleonasm: using more words than are necessary is another danger faced and often not avoided: evidence is in the multi-volume or excessively flatulent autobiographies of some of the rich and famous.
5 Libel: anything published which could be interpreted as a false statement damaging to a person's reputation is a libel. If deliberate, the libel is criminal; if not criminal, defamatory words can (and do) lead to civil actions. Some care, therefore, needs to be taken in writing about the behaviour of others.

These then are some of the dangers. They are there to be heeded if the writer is seeking eventual publication. They can be ignored by those of you who are not seeking fame. A simple letter is a form of autobiography; so too is a youngster's essay on 'what I did in the holidays'. If you are writing for private view only, none of these strictures apply: you can write what you like in as many words as you like.

Range and depth

There are several forms of autobiography. **Letters** to family, friends, lovers, business colleagues and even publishers is one. Letter-writing is personal: it is likely to contain news of one's activities or views on public or private events. Letters therefore qualify as an autobiographical voice.

Since a **diary** presents a private view of events, it also qualifies. Many writers never proceed past the stage of diary-writing, finding it a satisfying mode of self-expression.

A more formal kind of diary is a **journal**: among the famous are the journals of James Boswell, the biographer of Dr Samuel Johnson. They tend to be more literary than diaries, and record events rather than daily episodes.

Lastly, there's the deliberate attempt to write one's own **autobiography** or **memoirs**. If you take a look along the shelves in your local public library, you'll see a wide range of autobiographies written by 'personalities' who have made careers in the theatre, films, sport, television, business.

Their depth and merit vary: some performers unexpectedly find they are skilful writers — Dirk Bogarde and John Mortimer are two. Others lack sufficient skill and confidence to compose alone and a 'ghost writer' is brought in to assist, or an editor has to work very hard to transform dull prose into lively anecdotes. However, these are autobiographies that have been published; your ambitions may be more modest, that is to write about your life without expecting to expose your work to public gaze.

Activity

This activity is a preparation for your own writing. Having listed the four main types of autobiography, go to the public library and pick out one, two or more books of letters, journals, diaries and personal autobiographical histories. Read them in full or in part, thinking about the purposes of the writer and the skills that they have employed.

Letter-writing

We could put letters into three broad categories — formal, informal and personal. Formal means business letters: creativity may well feature in them as in a copywriter's description of the advantages of a certain product but for the purposes of this book we shall exclude them; there are plenty of other books on how to write effective business letters. Informal could include letters written for reading by more than one person and possibly even published — letters to clubs, societies and colleagues. The third group are personal letters to friends, family, lovers. Let's concentrate on this group.

As in any form of communication, a letter is distinguished (or not) by its content, style and message. Style is personal: informality and the personality of the writer are perfectly acceptable. Most people like to receive letters: if the receiver is lonely or away from home a letter becomes very important indeed. Therefore personality is a key factor and this is shown both in style and content — perhaps the grammar isn't correct, perhaps the logic of events isn't entirely accurate, perhaps someone's reputation is mutilated. All are acceptable traits. Some letters read as if they were spoken language, a continuation of the writer's conversation, spotted with exclamation marks, capitals and underlining for emphasis. For private reading, this is acceptable. If however, letters are for publication, one might be more careful on content and style. Excessive emphasis with capital letters or exclamation marks is generally frowned on by editors. You have, therefore, to decide whether to write for posterity or for private view.

Another virtue of letter-writing is that it enables some people to express their views more openly. It is a means of self-expression: many people are able to put emotions, feelings and opinions on paper much more easily than they can through speech.

Letters are also a means of sharing experiences. They are an essential lifeline between family and friends, especially if separated by seas and continents. They also present personal reactions or attitudes to events, thus recording emotions and memories.

This list of the special qualities of letters is important because it indicates that letters have all the integral aspects of autobiography. Let us summarize these qualities:

1 A vital **communication** link between people.
2 A factual **record** of happenings, memories, people.
3 An opportunity for emotional release or to explore feelings and thus to be a kind of **therapy**.

4 A **creative outlet** for the expression of opinions and personal views.

Activity

It will not come as a major surprise that this assignment is to write a letter. The topic is left open for you — a family event, a holiday, a wedding, birthday etc, or a subject that is more 'official' involving business in some way. You should, however, try to incorporate the four elements listed above. The letter need not be more than, say, four A4 sides, and it can be in any style that is a style that you personally feel confident with. When finished, you should try to discuss your letter with a tutor, colleague or friend.

Diaries

Personal diaries could be divided into four main categories:

1 Business desk diaries recording meetings, events and decisions, open to public gaze.
2 Semi-public diaries for briefcases and handbags with meetings, birthdays and other family or social activities.
3 Strictly private diaries in which people enter not only events but their feelings about them and about people.
4 Diaries of the famous or action-men and action-women, kept with the intention of eventual publication.

For this book, we shall concentrate on categories 2 and 3. They provide rich opportunities for creative writing for, although the events need to be factually correct, the observations and the style in which they are made are entirely personal.

Activity

In an earlier activity, it was suggested that you might visit a local library and look at various forms of autobiography. On the next occasion, concentrate on published diaries. Ask a library assistant to help by selecting three or four published diaries. Read extracts from them. Analyse them in terms of:

1 Content — events, happenings, people mentioned in them.
2 Personal reflections and opinions — what do they tell you about the character or personality of the writer.
3 Writing style — is it formal, informal, chatty, stylized, for private or public gaze.

Autobiographies

As with letters and diaries, there are no strict rules for writing an autobiography apart from the law of libel. It is free expression of the story of your life. The difficulties are not usually in seeking the right words and selecting the appropriate event, but in digging deep into one's own persona and psyche. This can be a painful process — too agonizing for some people who prefer to take refuge in writing through a third person ('he' or 'she' instead of 'I') or who fictionalize their experiences.

Activity

Imagine that you are going to write the story of your life, in full or in part. What difficulties can you see?

True or false?

Among the difficulties you may have spotted are:

1. **Honesty** — will you tell a story strictly as it happened, or with embellishments or omissions that put you in the best light?
2. **Reliability** — if you are writing about the past, are your facts accurate? Don't always trust your memory — try to establish facts by research.
3. **Distance** — one problem of distance is time: is your memory accurate? Another is distance from people. For example, other members of your family or your friends are likely to view you and your life differently. Will you take account of this, or ignore it?
4. **Deletion** — are you likely to delete facts or events that disparage other people or are damaging to your own self-esteem or reputation?
5. **Falsity** — which opens the door to the law of libel.

Activity

Rather than write your complete life-story, pick on one event or episode from the past that was important to you. Write about it. At this stage don't be too anxious about style, syntax, grammar. Write it freely in, say, no more than four pages of A4. When you have finished, give it to a member of the family or a friend(s) for comment. How does it match up to the four major difficulties listed earlier?

Writing skills

One could approach autobiographical writing by learning from and adapting the styles of famous practitioners — politicians, sportsmen and women, entertainers. Learn — yes, but adapt, that's dubious. As you'll see from your reading, style reflects personality. People who write in a pompous way are likely to have been fairly boring throughout their lives. But even if you write humorously, insultingly, mockingly, pompously, there's skill in it.

These skills are the same as they are for other forms of writing — clarity, correctness, variety. You must catch and hold the reader's attention.

All this advice is looking to publication: if you are writing for your family or yourself, the skills are just as important but can be given freer rein.

A model

'Enchantingly witty . . . it should be held as the model for all autobiographies of our times.'

What an accolade. Wouldn't we all love this to be said of our work. Instead, it was written by Auberon Waugh (himself the author of an amusing autobiography, *Will This Do?*) of John Mortimer's *Clinging to the Wreckage*.

Read this extract from John Mortimer's book. It describes how (long before Rumpole of the Bailey was ever thought of) he replaced Laurie Lee as scriptwriter to the Crown Film Unit.

'Laurie Lee is an enormously talented writer who can find more ingenious ways than most people of putting off the appalling moment of putting pen to paper. When he has made coffee, filled his pipe, changed his typewriter ribbon, moved the furniture, telephoned his mother, had a sleep, gone for a walk, he is often reduced to copying out the newspaper. I don't know if he found this rate of progress perfect for poetry, but his poetic prose created difficulties in the documentary film world. Perhaps his heart was still in Spain where he had walked the dusty roads from village to village, drinking with the soldiers and playing his fiddle to pale girls with tragic eyes. At any rate the sound of his recorder was heard less often in the corridors and in time it was learned that there was to be a vacancy in the script department.

After what seemed a lifetime as an assistant director I was called into the office of the new Head of the Crown Film Unit, an extremely kind man who looked at me sadly.

'We were wondering,' he said gently, 'whether you were exactly cut out by nature to be an assistant director. I mean, Doris says you're having a bit of trouble saying "Quiet please".'

'Just a bit.' I had to admit it.

'When I was an assistant director I was on my toes the whole time. I mean, are you quite sure *you* are?'

'Well. Not the whole time. No.'

'Bit of trouble, Doris tells me, getting the electricians to Liverpool?'

'I did find them in the end.'

'But you shouldn't ever have lost them. Isn't that the point? You know, it seems very hard to me to actually *lose* an electrician.'

I might have said that if he thought that he didn't know our hourly boys. Instead I looked suitably contrite.

'Doris and I have gone over the situation from every possible point of view and the conclusion we've come to is that you're not exactly a "natural" as an assistant.'

'Not a "natural", perhaps.'

'Look, you are a writer, aren't you?'

I had had one story published in the *Harrovian* and one in *Lilliput*. I secretly cherished half a novel about the Crown Film Unit which I was writing between takes. 'Oh yes,' I said. 'I'm a writer.'

'There's going to be a vacancy in the script department when Laurie goes. The idea we've arrived at, that is Doris and I have arrived at it, is that we should all be a great deal better off with you in the script department. Script-writers have almost never been known to lose the electricians. Look, we'll send you off somewhere to write a script and then you can show it to Laurie and if he passes it you're on.'

I went to the door in a sort of dream. My first novel may have been unpublishable, but now I was a writer; my pay-packet would say so just as my battledress shoulder-flash said 'Crown Film Unit'. Only when I got to the door did a doubt cross my mind.

'Where will you send me off? To write a script, I mean.'

If the Head of the Unit was laughing to himself he had the mercy not to show it. 'I don't know,' he said. 'What about Watford Junction?'

I went to Watford on a bicycle and spent a day staring at the railway lines and the rolling-stock without inspiration. Then I went home and wrote a script, based on the movies I had admired (*La Femme du Boulanger* and *La Bête Humaine*), about a station-master's wife and her unhappy love affair with a GI in charge of an American Army Transport Post. I sat by the fire after dinner and read it aloud to my father, doing the characters in various voices.

'When the war's over,' he said when I'd finished, 'I think you ought to take the bar exams. I think that would be a wise precaution.'

Biography

With a biography, we are still on the same subject — people. One advantage it has over autobiography is that biography is about someone else, and therefore possibly less wounding, less worrying to write. However, biography does need different skills. One is research: writing about yourself comes mainly from your memory; other people's lives are based on numerous witnesses who should be questioned (if still alive) or their memoirs read (if published or in private letters).

Writing biography can be a very enjoyable business — the research, the piecing together of evidence, the conversations with others, the writing itself. It can also be very laborious: people spend years on someone else's life.

There are a number of points to be considered when writing biographical material:

- **Length**: Consider, before you begin, approximate length — perhaps a short (200 to 500 words) essay about a member of your family; or a full-length (300 pages) study.
- **Aims and readers**: Before you write, be clear about aims — is the 'life' to be set against the social or political or military history of the times; will it be for a specific group of readers or for general reading?
- **Sequence**: Will you begin at the beginning (birth) and proceed chronologically or will you structure it to jump about in a time sense?
- **Alternative views**: Will it be only your view of the subject (victim?) or will you have the views and opinions of others about this person and the times they lived in?
- **Accuracy**: It is hoped that careful research will ensure that facts are reported accurately; if not, the same hazard that was noted earlier — libel — could spell danger.

Remember that your readers need to be sufficiently aroused to maintain their interest, so your writing has to be as skilful for biography as it is for fiction or non-fiction writing.

Activity

Attempt a short biographical piece. Pick on a subject, alive or dead, family or friend, famous or infamous and write no more than 800 words on an episode or a period in this person's life. Discuss your writing with a friend or tutor.

Summary

You have seen in this unit that:

- there are distinctive skills in writing autobiographical and biographical material
- whatever the subject, research is essential to correct infirm memories or find out more about the subject
- there are all kinds of writing that give opportunities for the development of writing skills, including letters, diaries, essays, biographies.

You ought to have practised some of these skills by completing the activities and the linked assignment, benefiting from the practice and a tutor's comments.

Assignment 4

To be attempted after completing Unit 8.
Time guide: 3 hours

My Own Story

You should choose a subject for an autobiographical or a biographical treatment. If it's you (autobiography), you can select a diary or journal entry, a letter or a chapter from your (as yet) unpublished autobiography. If your choice is a biography, select the lucky person carefully for you need to interview him or her, or be able to interview and question other people about the person.

You don't have to write a volume. Let's say one chapter, one episode, one letter, one diary entry. But with sufficient length and depth to give some opportunity to demonstrate your skill. Set a maximum of 1000 words, perhaps less, 500 words up to 1000. Write your copy for Assignment 4 carefully and when completed, you could ask someone to read and comment on it, or use it as part of a course.

UNIT 9

PLAYS

Objectives

After working through this unit you should be better able to:
- appreciate the limited commercial markets for plays
- decide whether or not to write for personal and private reading
- write dialogue and set stage directions
- share your experience of writing plays with other people, and listen to their assessment of your work.

The play's the thing

It's a tall order to ask someone to write a play if they've never attempted it before. Most dramatists, scriptwriters or screenplay authors emerge from 'the trade'. That is they are or have been involved in the theatre, either as professionals or in amateur theatrical productions. By serving this apprenticeship, they have observed and thus have learned how a play is constructed and is performed. The best of them, namely William Shakespeare, was an actor. Perhaps it would be good advice to budding playwrights to persuade them to join a local community drama group, if they haven't already done so.

On the other hand, beginners aren't banned. You may have an original idea; you may have practised dialogue in front of a mirror or in the secret recesses of your bedroom or office; you may have already typed out the first scene. If all this applies to you, go on. You may have a masterpiece in draft. Or you could feel that you will burst unless you write a play. If so, do it.

This unit is designed for people in both categories — theatre-folk and beginners. But since it is only a unit and not a substantial book, it has been constructed only as an introduction, with hints on the skills rather than a detailed explanation of them. If you are dissatisfied with this approach, read a lot of plays, go to the theatre, study the specialist books mentioned at the end of this one, and write your play(s).

Find the market

Let's suppose that you are the new Alan Ayckbourn. You have a play exploding inside you, or it has already burst and you have a fully-written typescript. First, find a literary agent who handles plays: they are listed in the *Writers' & Artists' Yearbook*. An agent will give you good advice.

If not, you can try an independent approach. As a new unknown playwright, it's unlikely that *Miss Saigon* will immediately be dropped to fit in your play. A London West End opening is unlikely. Therefore, try a local company that is known to be interested in putting on plays by new authors; better still, local new authors. How? You write to the company, include a synopsis, size of cast and some details of the sets and whether music is needed or not. Ask for the play to be read. That's the start. If it's read, you'll get an opinion.

Alternatively, there are playwriting competitions that you could enter. Some have prizes. However, the most likely route to a market is to join a local company, make your mark, and then offer your play for reading — and if good enough — performance. In all of these operations take care both of your typescript and your copyright. Always have a spare photocopy with your name on it, in case of loss.

The theatres and agents that market plays are in the *Yearbook*. If successful, there's another possible financial return. Many plays are published, for school use and for local dramatic societies, and copies are sold in the same way as novels to libraries and through bookshops. A successful play can sell 20 000 copies in hardback and paperback. There is also a market for radio and television plays as described in the unit on broadcasting.

If all else fails, you may be a member of a local community group who do not have ambitions about being published or West End fame. They may be perfectly happy to read and perform a play for amusement and expression. If you are part of this kind of social group, you've found your market.

Activity

Are you interested in writing a play(s)? If not, move on. If you are, what do you think are the factors that make an effective play?

One way to answer this question is to read some plays.

Here are the first few lines of a famous play, first performed 40 years ago and still featured in theatre repertoires.

JIMMY: Why do I do this every Sunday? Even the book reviews seem to be the same as last week's. Different books — same reviews. Have you finished that one yet?

CLIFF: Not yet.

JIMMY: I've just read three whole columns on the English Novel. Half of it's in French. Do the Sunday papers make you feel ignorant?

CLIFF: Not 'arf.

JIMMY: Well, you *are* ignorant. You're just a peasant. (*To Alison.*) What about you? You're not a peasant are you?

ALISON: (*Absently.*) What's that?

JIMMY: I said do the papers make you feel you're not so brilliant after all?

ALISON: Oh — I haven't read them yet.

JIMMY:	I didn't ask you that. I said —
CLIFF:	Leave the poor girlie alone. She's busy.
JIMMY:	Well, she can talk, can't she? You can talk, can't you? You can express an opinion. Or does the White Woman's Burden make it impossible to think?
ALISON:	I'm sorry. I wasn't listening properly.
JIMMY:	You bet you weren't listening. Old Porter talks, and everyone turns over and goes to sleep. And Mrs Porter gets 'em all going with the first yawn.
CLIFF:	Leave her alone, I said.
JIMMY:	(*Shouting.*) All right, dear. Go back to sleep. It was only me talking. You know? Talking? Remember? I'm sorry.
CLIFF:	Stop yelling. I'm trying to read.
JIMMY:	Why do you bother? You can't understand a word of it.
CLIFF:	Uh huh.
JIMMY:	You're too ignorant.
CLIFF:	Yes, and uneducated. Now shut up, will you?
JIMMY:	Why don't you get my wife to explain it to you? She's educated. (*To her.*) That's right, isn't it?
CLIFF:	(*Kicking out at him from behind his paper.*) Leave her alone, I said.
JIMMY:	Do that again, you Welsh ruffian, and I'll pull your ears off. He bangs Cliff's paper out of his hands.
CLIFF:	(*Leaning forward.*) Listen — I'm trying to better myself. Let me get on with it, you big, horrible man. Give it me. (*Puts his hand out for paper.*)
ALISON:	Oh, give it to him, Jimmy, for heaven's sake! I can't think!

Did you recognize it? It is the first lines of *Look Back in Anger* by John Osborne, introducing Jimmy Porter, the archetype for the 1950s 'angry young men'.

Why choose it?

This is the play's opening scene. There's no waiting, no measured and calm introduction to the setting, the characters, the plot. Jimmy Porter immediately launches into a furious attack on Alison and Cliff, gripping the audience immediately with his verbal violence. Notice how Jimmy interrogates them: Cliff and Alison stonewall their replies but Jimmy thunders on, with each of his lines an insult. There's the power and in the hands of competent actors, the first scene explodes.

Lessons to be learned

There are specific skills in writing plays just as there are for other forms.

First, the **theme** or **idea**.

An audience wants to know what a play is **about**. They might get a hint from the title: *Loot* or *Lady Windermere's Fan* or *The Merchant of Venice* give broad clues.

But, at the end of the performance, an audience may carry away not a remembered theme but a response — they may have laughed at humour; they could be saddened by a tragedy; they might have been impressed by the sets, costumes, music. There are two lessons here — **theme** and **impression**.

Next, there's **structure**. Some critics say that a play should have a start, middle and end: if in three acts, the three parts could be in sequence. Or not. A play can start with the ending, and work backwards. But, whatever the shape of the play, it does require a structure that the audience understands by the time they reach final curtain.

However, since a play is in spoken language, the features that impress are **characters** and **dialogue**. The conversations and speeches must give actors opportunities to display their talents. If you read some plays, you'll see that only occasionally are there stirring speeches, monologues or brilliant lines. Most of the dialogue is in exchanges, with one or more characters reacting to each other as well as to outside events. One of the reasons for the great success of Alan Ayckbourn's plays is that in a prosaic domestic setting, such as a kitchen, a bedroom, a party, characters react in extraordinary ways. Couples are mismatched, eccentric, puzzled, bewildered — not by events but by each other. The result — hilarity (and often sadness)— that keeps an audience attentive and appreciative of the talent that created these scenes.

Summarizing, then, the skills required of a play are:

- a theme or idea which is worked through the plot of the play
- an emotional response from the audience
- structure, pattern, sequence and a conclusion
- interesting characters who reveal themselves through dialogue
- reaction between characters
- pace and style
- an opportunity for actors to give a performance that arouses the interest of the audience.

Get all of these right and it could mean your early West End debut.

Activity

We all need a stimulus. Choose one of these:

1   an episode that you observed or took part in
2   a picture in a newspaper or magazine
3   a character you admire, or dislike, or are amused by.

Write a page of dialogue based on this stimulus. You must have two characters, perhaps more. The activity is designed to give practice in dialogue: if you enjoy it, write more — 2, 3 or more pages. Read the dialogue aloud with a friend — this is an effective way of avoiding a false ring to spoken words.

Plot, events, storyline and characters

Theme, idea, plot. These are called the play's **elements**. They are woven together to create the atmosphere, events, characters and impact of the play.

The **plot** needs careful preparation. The plot is the plan, the map, of the play. Before a line or a word are written, it is suggested that the plot is worked out. Seeing a plot as a map is a useful exercise. A playwright can start anywhere on the map — at the destination (last scene), the middle, or at the beginning (Act 1, Scene1). Wherever one starts, however, the map should be largely drawn before the events of the play are decided on. One way to plot the play is to have a page or two for each act and to work out in rough the sequence of main events or topics which take the play (and the audience) from curtain up to curtain down.

Events are the happenings in a plot. They are the dramatic occurrences or verbal exchanges that move the play on its journey. The traditional method of sequencing events was in scenes; in some Shakespeare plays there are many scenes, each one a hook to carry one or more events. Traditionally, too, scenes are grouped into acts, with any number from two to four acts as a recognisable pattern. However these are conventions, not requirements. Some experimental dramatists write in a continuous flow or deliberately upset sequence so that a play begins with its final conclusion and then lets the rest of the play tell the story. There are conventions, then, on plot, events, theme and idea but you don't necessarily have to adopt or apply them. Be an experimental dramatist if you wish.

Storyline is the method by which action develops. 'Action' doesn't mean fights or riots. It could be verbal interchanges between characters or physical actions. Inevitably **conflict** will arise. Conflict leads to action — there's a new situation, a more complicated problem, all requiring responses from people.

Having roughly decided on the plot and its development you have to introduce characters. In your preliminary notes, draw up a list, adding a few words to describe them — their clothes, age, demeanour, attitudes. Sometimes playwrights give very little information, allowing actors and directors to make their own interpretation. Other writers give detailed instructions.

Scene-setting describes place and time: 'Saturday evening, about 7pm, in the living room of the McLeish's house', or 'The castle at Elsinore; a winter's day'. Instructions can be brief, or extensive: there's no set rules, only the playwright's personal judgement.

Activity

Imagine that you are to write a play set in a suburban house or flat, in a style similar to that of Arnold Wesker, Alan Ayckbourn or Harold Pinter. You could model the scene on your own home, or that of a friend or neighbour. Write the stage directions and brief descriptions of three characters introduced in Act 1.

Review activity

So far, you have been set activities that ask you to write some dialogue, stage directions and character definitions. However, the pace and style of a play are the factors that give it substance. Characters do not stand still; their conversation creates and develops the plot. Suddenly, as in a Joe Orton or a Harold Pinter play, characters erupt after what appears to be inane, desultory remarks. Other writers such as Tom Stoppard and Oscar Wilde gave their characters a voice and speeches to accelerate the action.

The review activity suggests that you try to apply these skills. Read some plays: collected editions are available in most public libraries. Then write a full act for a play: it could be a one-act play, or one of three acts. Either way, your work should include these elements:

- a title
- scene-setting: place and time
- brief character descriptions
- stage directions: furniture, entrances, positioning of actors, sound, lighting or musical effects.

Then write the dialogue, with any other stage directions that are necessary.

You might discuss your play with a friend, or a member of the family, or your tutor.

UNIT 10

POETRY

Objectives

After working through this unit you should be better able to:
- appreciate some of the problems as well as the fascination of writing poetry
- write some poetry in one or more of its different forms
- share your experience of writing poetry with other people.

Poetry

In contrast with playwriting which demands performance, poetry is a solitary, private activity. It is also on the increase: poetry reading and writing are encouraged at school and since the disciplines are not to write in the style of Shelley or Byron but to seek a simpler, more direct style and voice, more people than one might imagine try their hand at verse.

Practitioners may be numerous but publishers are not. There are some enlightened ones: Faber, Bloodaxe Books and Penguin are three notable examples. But financial reward for newcomers is unlikely; Keats, Betjeman, Tennyson, Milton, T. S. Eliot, and other famous poets might still earn a crumb but John or Janet Jones would find it difficult to secure the approval and support of a modern publisher.

Lack of fame is no deterrent. People write poetry privately; if their words, phrases, rhymes and sounds find an audience that thinks, feels and admires, that's a bonus. If you want to share your enthusiasm with others, there are local poetry-reading and writing societies (the public library will have details) or there's the Poetry Society and the Poetry Library — their addresses and of other organizations are in the *Writers' & Artists' Yearbook*, along with details of competitions and awards.

Read first, write second

You must read some poetry before you write any. Not to copy the style of other poets. But simply to see the range of subjects, styles, approaches. Mix the classics with contemporary poets. If you haven't many books of poetry on your own shelves, go to the library — you will be surprised at the range and, if you are daunted, just one anthology may be enough to get you started.

Anthologies or collections of poems by different writers are valuable because they demonstrate different styles. If you find a poet that you enjoy or admire, you should then seek out a book of poems by this writer. You could go further and model your first efforts on this writer: you won't be accused of copying because every poet's voice is different in one way or another.

Activity

Having enjoyed reading one or more poets, reflect on why you prefer their work.

Skills audit

Among the many ideas you may have singled out, these could be included:

- **Subjects** — Do your favourite poets write on topics that appeal to you such as the countryside, places, seasons, family, emotional conflicts, flowers, etc?

- **Rhymes** — Do rhythms of words and phrases make a special appeal?

- **Language** — Is the poet's choice of language appropriate and attractive?

- **Structure** — Does the flow and order of the poetry impress you with its precision and accuracy?

- **Discipline** — Being more confined and restricted by poetic conventions, a poem needs discipline — did you recognize it?

- **Poetic form** — Do you particularly favour a particular form of poetry — odes, sonnets, rhyming couplets, free verse, love poetry?

- **Feeling** — Above all, perhaps, a poem creates a response because of the feelings it expresses or arouses in the reader — was this true in your case?

These factors — one or more of them — make poetry a distinctive creative writing form. And, despite the difficulties in writing poetry, many, many people enjoy writing and reading poems.

More poetry, please!

Let's look at some examples.

First, **subject.**

Sylvia Plath who was married to another poet, Ted Hughes, died tragically at the age of 32. Many of her poems are anguished, but not this one on a prosaic subject, mushrooms. Rhymes are dispensed with, but there is a clear structure and language and feeling (even for mushrooms!) are distinctive.

Mushrooms
Overnight, very
Whitely, discreetly,
Very quietly

Our toes, our noses
Take hold on the loam,
Acquire the air.

Nobody sees us,
Stops us, betrays us;
The small grains make room.

Soft fists insist on
Heaving the needles,
The leafy bedding.

Even the paving.
Our hammers, our rams,
Earless and eyeless,

Perfectly voiceless,
Widen the crannies,
Shoulder through holes. We

Diet on water,
On crumbs of shadow,
Bland-mannered, asking

Little or nothing
So many of us!
So many of us!

We are shelves, we are
Tables, we are meek,
We are edible,

Nudgers and shovers
In spite of ourselves.
Our kind multiplies

We shall by morning
Inherit the earth.

Our foot's in the door.

Activity

What is your response to this poem? Is it effective in giving mushrooms a voice? Do the short lines and short verses work? Is the choice of language appropriate?

Second, **rhyme.**

Choosing to write in rhyme is a personal decision. Beginners think that poetry must rhyme. Not so. However, many writers (and readers) prefer rhymes because they provide a recognizable framework for theme, ideas, discipline, feeling — that is, other elements of poetry.

But there's another discipline: rhymes have to be appropriate, relevant. Because you write about a deer, you don't have to (and perhaps shouldn't, unless you are creating a nonsense or humorous rhyme) choose rhyming words such as beer, fear, weir, disappear, tier and so on! Poets who write in rhymes start with such a list — a long list — and then select rhymes that are relevant to their subjects. They also decide on where a rhyme should appear: at the end of a line, in the middle or at the start of a line, on every second line, the last two lines, or other variations.

Roger McGough is another twentieth century writer, but of a vastly different style — 'laconic, ironic, Byronic' (that is Laurie Lee's rhyming assessment).

A Joy to be Old

It's a joy to be old.
Kids through school,
The dog dead and the car sold.

Worth their weight in gold,
Bus passes. Let asses rule.
It's a joy to be old.

The library when it's cold.
Immune from ridicule.
The dog dead and the car sold.

Time now to be bold.
Skinnydipping in the pool.
It's a joy to be old.

Death cannot be cajoled.
No rewinding the spool.
The dog dead and the car sold.

Get out and get arse'oled.
Have fun playing the fool.
It's a joy to be old.
The dog dead and the car sold.

Structure

Stevie Smith was another unique talent, a poet and novelist who worked as a secretary for a publishing company. Read 'The Jungle Husband'.

The Jungle Husband
Dearest Evelyn, I often think of you
Out with the guns in the jungle stew
Yesterday I hittapotamus
I put the measurements down for you but they got lost in the fuss
It's not a good thing to drink out here
You know, I've practically given it up dear.
Tomorrow I am going alone a long way
Into the jungle. It is all grey
But green on top
Only sometimes when a tree has fallen
The sun comes down plop, it is quite appalling.
You never want to go in a jungle pool
In the hot sun, it would be the act of a fool
Because it's always full of anacondas, Evelyn, not looking ill-fed
I'll say. So no more now, from your loving husband, Wilfred.

A poet's pack

One way to write poetry is to begin with a blank page and a blank mind and take off from there, allowing free rein to inspiration.

Another way is first to study the skills of poetry-writing before putting pen to paper. There's a very useful book on the tools of this trade, *The Way To Write Poetry* (see the booklist). Written by Michael Baldwin, himself a poet, it covers the basic ground rules and contains dozens of valuable hints.

First, a poem has an idea, a theme, a **concept**. It may, or may not, have **rhymes**. Some rhyme patterns have already been described. Another addition to the poet's pack is **alliteration**, the repetition of the same letters. Used sparingly it is musical, as in a Laurie Lee poem:

Blown bubble-film of blue, the sky wraps round
Weeds of warm light whose every root and rod
Splutters with soapy green, and all the world,
Sweats with the bead of summer in its bud.

Overdone, it grates:

Big and burly Bertha
Wears B.O. and Brut.

Poetry is a kind of music, so another element is **rhythm**. Not the same as rhyme, rhythm can be judged by reading a poem or listening to one being read. It is the musical quality: as in a concerto or opera, one wrong note or badly sung word can spoil the performance. When rhythm is organized it becomes **metre**. These are formal, systematically arranged, patterns of words determined by measure. There is a variety of metres — hexameters, pentameters and others for more advanced forms of poetry. If you intend to move towards advanced forms of writing, you will need to study meter.

Activity

Make an attempt at writing a short poem with rhymes. It can be verse of your own choosing or even in the form of a limerick such as:

George Stephenson said: 'These repairs
Are costing a fortune in spares.
I'll be out of pocket
When I've finished this Rocket,
Unless British Rail raise their fares.

More poetic forms

Having successfully written your first rhymes, you could go on to more sophisticated word-patterns.

Imagery is the technique of using 'images', that is phrases that create a mood or picture in the mind. Keats, Shelley, Wordsworth, Hardy, Yeats — all were exceptional users of imagery. For example, using a favourite:

I wandered lonely as a cloud
That floats on high o'er vales and hills,
When all at once I saw a crowd,
A host, of golden daffodils,
Beside the lake, beneath the trees,
Fluttering and dancing in the breeze.

What images are conjured up? Countryside, sky, flowers, lakes, mountains — the essence of the Lake District.

Alliteration has been mentioned. Another technique is **assonance** — it appears in Wordsworth's poem, that is the repetition of the same vowel sound at least twice and generally more often, as in

'A host of golden daffodils'

Count the 'o's.

Another clever use of words is in **onomatopoeia**, a long word to describe short ones that reflect or imitate the sound of the word as in 'fizz', 'hiss', 'yelp', 'moo', 'crash'.

Poets love metaphor and simile. **Metaphor** is a method of describing one thing in terms of something else:

Love is a flame,
A city, and we have built it, these and I.
An emperor — we have taught the world to die.

Whatever love is, it can hardly be a flame, or a city or an emperor, but Rupert Brooke uses these nouns to give love a special quality, by association of ideas.

A **simile** make a comparison, by using the words 'like' and 'as'. In Wilfred Owen's poem of 1914–18 soldiers:

Bent double, like old beggars under sacks,
Knock-kneed, coughing like hags . .'

Activity

Again, try it. Read some poems, then try your hand at a few lines which use one or more of these poetic forms and techniques.

Free verse

Free verse is what it says — verse that is free from rhyme or meter. You could think that it is therefore easier to write. Wrong. In free verse (as in rhyme) every word must count, must be made to work. Success depends on whether the words — each word, each line — contributes to build the total picture of the idea or theme of the poem.

The room was suddenly rich and the great bay-window was
Spawning snow and pink roses against it
Soundlessly collateral and incompatible:
World is suddener than we fancy it.

Louis MacNeice was not an easy poet to read but he set a pattern for free verse that many modern poets have followed. It is a poetic form that appeals to many new writers and poets, and it may be the answer to your poetic inspiration.

Activity

Choose a subject and make an attempt to write a short poem in free verse style.

Further reading

Plays

Good advice on the markets for stage plays, radio and television plays and screenplays is given in the *Writers' & Artists' Yearbook*. Among several 'how to . . .' books, these two are suggested:

Steve Gooch, *Writing a Play*, A & C Black
Tom Gallacher, *The Way to Write for the Stage*, Elm Tree Books.

Poetry

It is essential to read the Poetry section of the *Writers' & Artists' Yearbook* (A & C Black) for a booklist, competitions, publishers' addresses, national and local societies. Among many books about writing poetry, these are recommended:

Michael Baldwin, *The Way to Write Poetry*, Elm Tree Books
Alison Chisholm, *The Craft of Writing Poetry*, Allison and Busby

There isn't space to suggest many collected editions but one that can be recommended is Fleur Adcock, editor, *20th Century Women's Poetry*, Faber & Faber. Among many anthologies are the Oxford series which include *English Traditional Verse, War Poetry, Satirical Verse* and others. Penguin's collection includes *Romantic Verse, Victorian Verse, Ballads* and others.

Review activity

Having worked your way through the poetry section of this unit, you ought to be in a position to compose a poem in one or more of the styles suggested. Choose your subject, select the poetic form (verse, free verse, sonnet or any other) and write a poem of a length of your choosing. You could ask a friend, colleague or tutor to read and comment on it.

Summary

In this unit you have been presented with two very different forms of creative writing, plays and poetry. As a consequence of studying this unit you should be in a better position to appreciate, understand and apply some of the disciplines within these sectors. And it may have given you an appetite which could be satisfied further by reading the specialist books listed here.

UNIT 11

WRITING FOR RADIO AND TELEVISION

Objectives

A creative writer can be working purposefully by staring out of the window or by walking the dog. Inspiration can come at any time and plots can be thought out while trudging across a hillside. Nevertheless, a writer who hopes to sell his or her work must eventually sit down and apply the rules. In this unit the rules are on writing for broadcasting. This unit is therefore designed to:

- identify the main disciplines and requirements needed by scriptwriters hoping to place their work in radio and television
- provide tasks and an assignment to give some practice in applying these skills and techniques.

Writing from experience

It is much more difficult to break into writing for broadcasting than it is to enter the world of journalism. In the first place, there are far fewer opportunities and outlets. For radio, there is the BBC, local radio (BBC and commercial) and networked independent radio. For television there is national and local BBC, ITV and Channel 4, plus Sky and other commercial channels. If your ideas or scripts for radio and television aren't accepted, where do you go next? On the other hand, an article you write for a magazine might have fifty possible outlets, and for your first novel or non-fiction book there could be over a hundred different publishers to approach. In the first place, therefore, it's difficult to break into this specialized market.

Other problems are concerned with expertise. Many television and radio writers and presenters fashion their skills as journalists on newspapers and magazines or as freelance writers commissioned to provide articles and stories. They have thus learned how to write effectively long before they seek out work in broadcasting.

Furthermore, radio and television look for experts. If you consider some popular factual topics — gardening, cooking, travel, music, sport — the writers/broadcasters are usually expert in their particular field, either as performers or as journalists.

This depressing picture doesn't entirely apply to fictional writing. Beginners do break in — but only if they show special talents for radio or television screenwriting, or if they are very lucky and are in the right place at the right time.

You could arrange your answer like this:

	Writer's knowledge and skill	Applied to suit radio broadcasts	Applied to suit television programmes
1	Specialist subject knowledge	Documentaries Talks Quizzes	Documentaries Feature programmes Quizzes
2	Good at dialogue	Plays	Plays
3	Historical research and/or biography	Educational broadcasting Documentaries Memoirs	Educational television Feature programmes such as antiques
4	Substantial expert with practical knowledge of 'how to . . .'	Feature programmes on how to furnish and decorate a home, play a particular sport, music, quizzes, etc.	An item for a magazine programme
5			
6			
7			
8			

What are your interests?

As you can see from the previous analysis, there are two kinds of knowledge and skills — writing skills and special subject knowledge.

Let us put writing skills to one side: they apply to all kinds of writing, with the additional requirement that you must know something about screenwriting.

Specialist knowledge — and the skills needed to translate your enthusiasm into a script and ultimately into a broadcast programme — is quite different. You really need to pick on a subject from your wide range of interests and concentrate on it through research, assembling information and structuring it into the format for a programme.

Activity

Here is a set of 'interests'. Suppose you can choose only three. Write 1, 2, 3 in the squares to indicate your interests or specialist knowledge in that order, 1 being your favourite interest or accomplishment, with 2 and 3 next in line.

☐	Wining and dining	☐	Jazz/folk music
☐	Pubs	☐	Classical music
☐	Sports	☐	Theatre
☐	Politics/history	☐	Watching TV
☐	Travelling	☐	Antiques
☐	Science	☐	Drinking
☐	Cinema	☐	Children
☐	Pets/animals	☐	Homemaking
☐	Pop music	☐	Gardening
☐	Dancing	☐	Countryside
☐	Keep fit	☐	Environmental concerns
☐	Technology	☐	Education
☐	Money	☐	Other (name it)

Who are your listeners or viewers?

Let us now turn to the skills of scriptwriting and screenwriting.

Assuming that you want to write for the broadcasting media, you must — as with all forms of writing — attract and hold the attention of your listeners or viewers. To do this, *you must write to please the audience, rather than yourself.*

You must ask yourself what does the audience expect from you. Your answer should include one or more of these:

- information
- a different viewpoint from theirs — that is, make them think
- entertainment
- discussion between two or more people with opposing or varied views.

The more you think about listeners and viewers, it will become more likely that you will hold their attention. A major problem is, of course, that viewers/listeners are of all ages, in all parts of the UK (and perhaps also overseas), and are unable to respond (unless you are involved in a phone-in programme).

Activity

To write for a vast invisible audience, you need to imagine that you have one listener or viewer sitting in front of you. In the same way that you would chat or talk easily to this single person (or a friend), you write the script. Avoid formal prose.

This activity has two parts. First, choose a topic or subject for, say, a five-minute item. Talk about it into a cassette recorder, putting your ideas and words in some kind of order or structure. Then, secondly, having played the recording, write out the episode or story or magazine item as if it would be broadcast.

On the first occasion that you practise and record your voice, you'll probably be horrified or at least uneasy about the nervousness in your voice. But you won't be broadcasting. Presenters and actors replace you. The importance of this exercise (activity) is to develop skill in translating or reproducing spoken language into written scripts or screenplays.

Writing for radio

The preparation you have done so far should have singled out one or more interests for one kind of radio programme — a magazine item perhaps or a full feature programme lasting 20 to 30 minutes. On the other hand, you may have decided to attempt a play or a short story that can be read out.

Magazine and feature programmes

This group includes full-length (up to sixty minutes) programmes; shorter items; two, three or up to five minute sketches; situation comedy material etc. Study the *Radio Times* and local radio programmes to see what is currently being produced and broadcast. If you want to take your ideas a step further, the thing to do would be to write a treatment or a synopsis which is a summary of the idea, then show in writing how this would be extended into a script that has an introduction or beginning, a sequence and a conclusion or resolution. A page or two of this material turned into a radio script would be useful.

Radio drama

If you think that you are quite good at writing dialogue (and, conversely, not outstanding with descriptive passages) then you could attempt a radio play. Each year over 400 plays are produced by the BBC, local radio stations and independent radio so there is a good market for radio drama. In addition, there is educational broadcasting which occasionally features short plays.

Most of this broadcast output is commissioned or is offered by established writers through their agents. However, there is always scope for new talent and good ideas either for a single play or a serial are welcome.

It will have occurred to you that radio is cheaper to produce that other broadcast forms because everything is told through sound. Nor is it necessary to have a large cast of voices. Sound engineers can produce background sounds such as traffic, aircraft, crowds, music and other requirements: the writer has to concentrate on the script.

Activity

Let's suppose that you are facing the discipline of writing a thirty-minute radio drama, and a blank sheet of white paper is staring at you in the typewriter.

Before you begin, what are the components of a radio drama. List them.

Story, people and action

Your list should include at least these three:

Story — radio listeners expect to be entertained, so a fairly strong story line is essential.

People — the story is told in sound, and the sound is made up of people's voices, so characterization should be strong.

Action — a story has to be told, so it would be reasonable to expect that the story has a theme which is developed through action — a conflict, a crisis or two, people reacting differently to events and each other, with eventually a resolution (the end). This is the traditional way of telling a tale and your treatment could be very different, for example by breaking up the time sequence of a story (such as by starting with the conclusion and telling the story in episodic sound bites) or as in a serial with the last line a cliffhanger for the next episode.

Language — the attention of a radio audience is caught and held by words, so every word has to count. Clever phrasing, aided by background effects (the sea, traffic, sobbing, laughter and so on) is essential.

Scriptwriting for radio

If you intend to submit your work to the BBC or a commercial company, there are a few rules about presentation.

Dialogue for a radio play is set out in much the same way as for a play. Characters' names can be typed in capitals on the left, the dialogue on the right of an A4 page. Directions for staging or atmospherics can be given at the beginning of a scene or in the margin and should be in capitals or italics. But directions are not important; radio producers are experts in knowing how to provide background. They judge a script by the quality of the writing.

Read All About It

There isn't space in this book to describe the different kinds of writing for radio. However, there are two books that explain in some detail how to plan, write and set out a script. These books are *Writing for Radio*, second edition, by Rosemary Horstmann, published by A & C Black and *The Way to Write Radio Drama* by William Ash, published by Elm Tree Books. These books contain examples of scripts for different purposes. Unlike television, where stage and locational settings have to be described, radio concentrates totally on spoken dialogue or commentary, so the quality of the writing dictates its acceptability, or not.

A brief example is given here to show you how to set out dialogue. However, if you hope to proceed further with writing for radio, you should consult the books mentioned and any others that you can obtain from your local bookshop or library.

Radio has made a vast contribution to comedy writing. This extract shows you how fast talking requires fast writing.

Mutt and Jeff

MRS JEFF:	Me, I had three.
MR MUTT:	Three what?
MRS JEFF:	Three children, you idiot.
MR MUTT:	What? All together?
MRS JEFF:	One after another — the usual way.
MR MUTT:	What did you call them, then?
MRS JEFF:	Tom, Dick and Harry.
MR MUTT:	All boys?
MRS JEFF:	No. All girls. But I like boys' names.
MR MUTT:	What about when they grow up?
MRS JEFF:	They are grown up. Our Dick's a model.
MR MUTT:	A model what?
MRS JEFF:	A model railway. With signals, stations, trains, that sort of thing.
MR MUTT:	I seem to have missed something.
MRS JEFF:	You missed the lot. You missed out completely on brains and when it was your turn for equipment, the storeman gave you a badly damaged set.

And so on.

Why choose it?

This extract is not a piece of evidence to illustrate high calibre writing for radio. The humour is crude and blunt and would require the two actors to use their very best voice skills to make it amusing. On the other hand, it is not unlike much of the output of comedy writing which looks uninspired when written down.

Which brings us to the vital ingredient of radio comedy (or drama or documentary), namely the voice. Ordinary material can be transformed by voices of distinction such as John Gielgud, Joyce Grenfell, Spike Milligan and many others. An actor's skill in using tone, range, emphasis, pauses and control can make a script come alive. A radio scriptwriter knows about these skills and should write and adapt his or her material to exploit an actor's brilliance. All of these skills would be needed to make the Mr Mutt and Mrs Jeff material come alive because the writing itself isn't very good.

Next, attitudes. Read the Mutt and Jeff piece again. What attitudes of mind, opinion and humour are displayed here?

What did you find?

Mr Mutt is portrayed as an idiot. Accidentally or deliberately, he misunderstands Mrs Jeff's answers. On the other hand, she deliberately turns the tables on him — three girls were given boys' names. Finally, in the last line, Mrs Jeff crudely insults Mr Mutt.

Funny? Well, it is singularly crude to read but in the hands of good actors, it could be amusing.

Dialogue coaching

You can see that for radio comedy and drama, dialogue is the crucial factor.

To be able to write effective dialogue is both a talent you are born with and a skill to be learned. The talent comes from the writer's own education, background, reading and attitude. The skills to be learned can be acquired by practice and by coaching. Practice simply means writing scripts, revising them, re-writing them, getting friends or actors to read them, and revising yet again. These skills can be coached. Attendance at a class on creative writing is one method of learning because a tutor will provide opportunities for writing, reading out loud and revising towards an acceptable final version. Other methods of 'coaching' are to attend a drama class or course at a local further education college and listen to the range of acting skills, or join a local dramatic society.

Viewpoint

Finally, viewpoint. This is what distinguishes one writer from another. Viewpoint is the way a writer approaches a plot, a situation, or dialogue. Is the intention to raise a laugh by making fun of other people (as in Mutt and Jeff). Or, at the other extreme, is it to praise the achievements of a famous person or persons; as in a documentary or biography. Viewpoint is personal — it distinguishes one writer from another and gives a distinctive set of opinions. Think of radio (and/or television) programmes on recent political leaders and their contribution to twentieth century history — Lenin, Churchill, Margaret Thatcher. Depending on the scriptwriter's viewpoint, the emphasis to the subject (the person) may be critical, approving, reflective, analytical, revisionist — depending on viewpoint.

Viewpoint, then, is a vital factor in writing for radio, television, novels, plays, poetry or any other creative form. It often provides an entrance gate to aspiring writers because it gives them an opportunity to attract the attention of a producer, an editor or a publisher and so break into one or more of the magic circles of creative (and published) writing.

Writing for television

A glance at the television pages in a Sunday or daily newspaper illustrates the range and the extent of television broadcasts. The list includes plays, serials, children's programmes, sporting events, game-shows and a profusion of 'light entertainment' which ranges from comedy half-hours to the Eurovision Song Contest. At any one time at peak evening viewing time an audience of between 10 and 20 million people are watching television. Awesome, isn't it?

Breaking in

It is difficult to break into radio scriptwriting, and the obstacles multiply for television writing. But it's not impossible. Again, as with radio, an apprenticeship served in journalism, screenwriting, the theatre, radio or as a novelist is a valuable preparation.

Activity

What do you think are the essentials for a television writer? Are they much different from radio? Make a short list of 'what you need'.

Scripts

1 No one can sell an **idea.** However, an idea should be on your list. On the other hand, anyone can have ideas and there's no copyright on them. But it's useful to start with one or two.
2 The same components are necessary for television dramas as for radio, that is **story, characters, action** and **response** — the elements of effective drama.
3 All this has to be transformed into a **script.** Now the list becomes more complex. A script needs dialogue and some stage instructions (place, time, the movement of people).
4 But there's a new factor — **visualization**. A script for drama, a game-show, a comedy, a magazine or feature programme — they all require a writer's ability to visualize and to influence the viewers to laugh, to share their emotions, to be puzzled — in short to be **involved.** Otherwise they switch off.

A visual medium

What should be apparent is that any script, for any audience, must have a strong visual impact. This requires a special kind of discipline. There's no point in writing 'Going out?' if a character puts on his cap or moves towards the door. And every word has to count: there's no room for extensive speeches or an unnecessary remark.

There isn't space in this book for lengthy explanation, with examples, of television scriptwriting. If you have ambitions in this field you should carefully study books written by experts: one of the best which is recommended to you is *Writing for Television* by Gerald Kelsey, published by A & C Black. As well as invaluable advice, it contains several lengthy scripts for drama, comedy and a serial.

Plots

Script editors and producers are unwilling to read lengthy scripts. They prefer to have a synopsis and a few scenes or episodes to see how a writer tackles the theme.

Before setting out, any television programme needs a plot. For a magazine programme a format would be a more appropriate word. Either way, it means the blueprint for a programme, a serial or a series. The plot, the storyline and the story synopsis have to be clear to the producer or editor before any decision could be made.

A detailed plot worked up into a two-page storyline enables a producer to visualize the scenes (indoor and outdoor), the size of the cast, the number of sets and, by putting costs on to each of these, an estimate of the total cost of production.

A plot synopsis

For example, here's the synopsis of a story that could be turned into a thirty- or sixty-minute drama. Eventually, after a great deal of discussion, alteration and many script changes and extensions, it became two one-hour episodes for a crime drama.

Deadly Nightshade

Background

The story is set in and dominated by a moorland. This could be Exmoor, a Yorkshire moor or in Scotland. The outdoor scenes would emphasize the wild terrain, fairly bare of trees, wind whistling, clouds racing. Other locations are in and around the moor — a pub, house interiors, police station. The atmosphere should combine this wild and beautiful but threatening environment with the storyline of a murderer on the loose.

Plot

A biological research institute is on the moor: the staff are concerned with the study of poisonous plants (thus the title); unknown at the start but emerging gradually as the story unfolds is that the research station also has a secret operation — deliberately growing plants with toxic capability. Why? This is all part of the story.

The drama begins with a young man trudging across the moor: this is Tom Hendrie who works for his father in a local shop, making and repairing furniture. Tom arrives home: it's early morning — very early — and it appears that he has been out on the moor since dawn. His wife, Liz, is still in bed. No children, and swiftly apparent there's a strained relationship between them. Why? Unknown now, slowly becomes apparent later. Tom is a leading character in the story, a major suspect in what happens later.

The second scene is of an attractive young woman on the moor; clad in anorak and jeans, she's studying plants on the ground. She becomes aware of a lurking presence and runs away, eventually arriving safety at the local village. The atmosphere of peril and potential violence is thus built up.

As the story unfolds, other characters are introduced. First the research institute with a female director — tensions with her staff and a relationship hinted at between Dr Joan McLaren (the director) and a male researcher, Jim Holt, who is questioning the work they are doing — hints here that the biological research has 'government' approval, but why?

Tom, on one of his solitary moorland walks, discovers the body of a young local girl, face contorted as if poisoned. This brings in a fresh group of characters — the police inspector, his assistant and a pathologist who suspects poisoning but cannot fathom its cause. Tom, because of his intense, withdrawn personality and inability to satisfy the police, becomes the main suspect. His wife, Liz, who we learn in flashbacks, has been unfaithful, has a fierce row with Tom, stalks out on the moor and is the second murder victim. Her body is found by Tom who leads the police to the moorland cave where her body lies.

The conflicts between the police and Tom, between Dr Joan McLaren and the staff of the Institute and a third murder culminate in a chase across the moorland and the capture of the poisoner, who after several twists and turns in the plot, turns out to be Jim Holt.

Storyline

This then is the synopsis. The producer or editor could be interested, even tempted, and may ask for a few pages of storyline on the full screenplay. This would contain dialogue and the basic locational and stage instructions. A marked-up example is shown in the next section of this unit.

Stage management

Stage instructions aren't part of the writer's job. Producers and directors often disregard instructions given in a screenplay or a treatment on where characters stand, how they behave and so on. They see stage direction as their responsibility, which it is.

However, it is wise to know about television production. The personnel work in teams. In **film** production the director is in charge of filming, aided by the producer or production manager (they handle administration, costings, correspondence and so on). The director is likely to have assistants and a stage manager — they look after props, actors and transport. In **television** production, there would be a producer, director and camera staff, plus production staff who include a stage manager and his or her assistants.

For a television production, the six stages are generally in this order:

1 Script approval and casting
2 Pre-production (setting scenes, finding locations, props and costumes)
3 Rehearsals — read-through (first reading) and subsequent rehearsals
4 Positioning cast and props on location
5 Production — filming on location or in the studio
6 Post-production — editing; adding music and sound effects; final film

A scriptwriter doesn't get involved in all these stages. But a script will be more professional if the author knows about them. To extend your knowledge, consult a very useful BBC guidebook, *BBC Television Training: Books Catalogue* which lists a series of useful books including *Television Stage Management* by Stephen Dinsdale.

The layout of a script

Another reason for describing the sequence is because a script should allow space for stage instructions. The text of a script should be typed on the right hand side of an A4 page, taking up to two-thirds of it. The correct type is capitals for names, locations and movements. On the left-hand side the producer or director adds production instructions. An example is given next of a script from a comedy programme; without production instructions.

SCRIPT

A ROOM WITHOUT A VIEW

SCENE 6 OFFICE LATE AFTERNOON

THE ROOM IS SMALL, UNTIDY, FILES AND BOOKS IN PILES. THERE'S A DESK WITH TYPEWRITER, PAPER STUCK IN IT. JUNE SITS AT THE TYPEWRITER, GAZING IN A HANDMIRROR, FIDDLING WITH HER HAIR.

DEREK COMES IN, WILSON BEHIND HIM.

DEREK: Hard at it again then, June?

JUNE: (INDIGNANT) I was here 'til eight o'clock last night.

DEREK: I'll have to speak to Charlie. He'll wear himself out.

WILSON: I'll give you a hand, June.

JUNE: You keep your hands to yourself. Anyway, shouldn't you be out digging ditches or something. You know, to keep your brain buzzing.

WILSON: Where's tomorrow's list, then?

The same script, with additional instructions for television production, is shown below

---

MARKED UP SCRIPT: Written and dialogue instructions

A ROOM WITHOUT A VIEW

SCENE 6 OFFICE LATE AFTERNOON

Props needed (see

separate Studio Props list)

THE ROOM IS SMALL, UNTIDY, FILES AND BOOKS IN PILES. THERE'S A DESK WITH TYPEWRITER, PAPER STUCK IN IT. JUNE SITS AT THE TYPEWRITER, GAZING IN A HANDMIRROR, FIDDLING WITH HER HAIR.

(1) D leads in, W closely behind, almost treading on his heels, stops halfway.

(1) DEREK COMES IN, WILSON BEHIND HIM.

DEREK: Hard at it again then, June?

(2) J sits at desk.

(2) JUNE: (INDIGNANT) I was here 'til eight o'clock last night.

DEREK: I'll have to speak to Charlie. He'll wear himself out.

(3) W comes behind J's desk, facing camera. J sits up, avoids W's leer.

(3) WILSON: I'll give you a hand, June.

JUNE: You keep your hands to yourself. Anyway, shouldn't you be out digging ditches or something. You know, to keep your brain buzzing.

(4) D advances to desk (see diagram).

(4) WILSON: Where's tomorrow's list, then?

Remember that the left hand column is someone else's job, but if a scriptwriter thinks about locations, character movement, camera positions and outcomes, and can give some instructions or clues, this all adds to the professionalism of the script and thus makes it more acceptable to a producer or editor.

If you are interested in writing for television or radio you should study the books mentioned in this unit.

Summary

In this unit and the linked assignment, you have considered, identified and produced ideas and scripts. In particular:

- the differences and variations in writing expertise required for scripts needed for broadcasts on radio and television
- the consideration of ideas based on your own interests
- the importance of matching script and particularly plot and dialogue to a large listening and viewing audience
- the structure and layout of scripts for radio and television.

Assignment 5

To be attempted after completing Unit 11.
Time guide: 4 hours

Radio or television script

Openings — or to put it more carefully — opportunities —- for freelance radio and television writers are not numerous. The unit on broadcasting has concentrated on drama, one-off radio and television plays. However, there are opportunities in other fields, such as feature or serial programmes. Serials are *The Archers*, *Brookside*, *Coronation Street* etc. Feature programmes are concerned with leisure or interest subjects — homes, gardens, antiques, animals, children, fashion, sport, documentaries and so on.

What you have to do for this assignment is first to choose a format — a drama, documentary, serial or any other format. Next, decide on the length: thirty, fifty, sixty minutes or longer. Having decided on your subject and its broadcast length, write a synopsis. It need not be lengthy but it should be complete, indicating the full extent of the programme: its objectives, characters and storyline. Secondly, having done the synopsis, write a page or two of script for any one scene or episode. This should contain stage instructions and dialogue (if a drama) or the script for the presenter or commentator.

When you have completed Assignment 5, ask (as before) a friend or a member of your family or a tutor to read and comment on it.

UNIT 12

NOVELS

Objectives

Novels incorporate all the elements of creative writing so far described; they are also unique in that a writer's skills have to be deployed at length and in a more complex way to capture and hold the interest of readers, and before this secure the approval of a publisher.

When you have completed this unit you should be able to:

* understand rather better the disciplines and the skills required to construct a novel
* plan the outline of a novel by writing a synopsis
* think and plan the theme, plot, characters and sequencing of a novel
* write at least a chapter of a novel, to better appreciate the range and depth of skills needed for this kind of writing.

Writing a novel — why do it?

Writing a novel is a very tough assignment. The job requires a combination of qualities that, in combination, most people lack. In the first place, there's commitment and time. Suppose you planned a modest novel of, say, 140 000 words. How long would it take you? If you could do it full-time with few other commitments, at a rate of, say, 1000 words a day, plus corrections and revisions, it might take anything between six months and a year. If you write part-time, much longer.

On the other hand, Barbara Cartland dictates her novels — and she's written over 600 — in three weeks flat.

Add in these personal qualities — perseverance, determination, resilience. A novel has to be conceived, planned, plotted, written and corrected. You'll need a strong will and persistence to last the distance.

Then there's imagination. You have to devise a plot (and sub-plots), characters, action, descriptions, dialogue — and over the full distance of 200 or more pages.

Having reached the finishing tape, with a typed script, the really hard part then begins — finding a publisher to take, or an agent to persuade a publisher to buy your work. This search can be very dispiriting. So some writers prefer to write for themselves alone or for their family.

On the other hand — and there are advantages — novel-writing is challenging and exciting and even if you never finish your novel there can be a lot of fun and satisfaction in trying it. One of the most oft-quoted clichés is that there's one story in all of us, the story of our life, so if you can fictionalize your own life-story this could be your first novel.

The other positive aspects are, of course, possible fame and fortune if your idea is successful, becomes a novel, and is enthusiastically published and promoted by a major company. Despite the modesty of authors, they do get huge satisfaction from seeing their work and their name in print.

Activity

The first activity in this unit is to try to decide whether or not you have the potential to be a novelist.
Dredge your mind and come up with some reasons — on paper — why you think you might be able to do it. Alternatively, if you have decided that a novel is not an attractive idea, list the reasons why not. By doing so and formulating the pros and cons, you may transform your viewpoint.

There's no right or wrong answer to this activity because the answer depends on your personal viewpoint. But you should have cleared your mind.

Activity

The next activity is to set you thinking about what's contained in a novel. Choose one that you've recently enjoyed reading. Try to think of six to eight **factors** or the **components** that made it a 'good idea'. List them in your notebook.

The golden mixture

Not all novels contain all these elements. But your list ought to contain some of them. Which ones are in your list?

1. **Category or genre** of the novel — crime, romance, thriller, western, etc.
2. **Plot** (and sub-plots) that make up the story
3. **Characters** — the main characters and sub-characters and how characters change and develop
4. **Action, dialogue and description** — the sequence, pace, and balance between descriptive and conversational writing
5. **Atmosphere and conflict** — suspense, excitement, tragedy; the relationship between people and events and relationships between people
6. **Viewpoint and style** — this is the combination of all the other factors plus control over and use of language to indicate your own personal style.

In future, as you read a novel, think about these aspects of the book: you'll become more critical of the novel, as do reviewers of books in the literary pages of newspapers. Reading is an important part of a novelist's continuing training: most famous novelists are avid readers, learning from other writers' work.

What happens now is that each of the general factors or components of a novelist's art will be described.

Category

Some writers specialize in a particular category: Frederick Forsyth for thrillers, Ruth Rendell for crime, and so on. Some able people can write for more than one category or genre.

Activity

Here are some of the main ones. Which one(s) appeal to you? Instead of a tick, list your preferences by writing the numbers 1 to 12 in the boxes, 1 being your likeliest chosen category, 12 the least likely.

	Crime/detective stories		Westerns
	Romance		Children's stories
	Historical fiction		Thrillers
	Science fiction		Travel
	Humour		Fantasy/occult
	Horror		Family histories
	Contemporary novels		Other (what is it?)

Plot

Let's take two examples.

Dragon Slayer is a famous children's novel by Rosemary Sutcliff. It was published by Penguin (Puffin) in 1966 and since then it has been reprinted almost every year so it could be judged a success.

It's a short novel, about 22 000 words in all. The story is based on Beowulf, the Anglo-Saxon hero. A summary or synopsis of the plot could be something like this:

A seafarer tells the tale of how, long ago, Grendel, the Man-Wolf monster, attacked and killed thirty of Hrothgar's warriors. Beowulf, 'with strength that could out-wrestle the great Northern bear' sets sail for the Danish court to volunteer as Hrothgar's champion. Beowulf fights and slays Grendel whose mother Death-Shadow-in-the-Dark vows revenge. In three great battles Beowulf fights and overcomes the monsters including the dragon that guards a treasure-hoard hidden away in the earth. But Beowulf is mortally wounded, dies and is given a hero's funeral.

This brief plot synopsis tells us nothing about the quality of the writing, the powerful imagination at work and the stirring, poetic style.

That's one plot. Briefly, look at two other novels, also by women writers. *Accident* by Danielle Steel is closely plotted. The action is an accident, a tragic accident and the novel explores how it effects many people and how they survive it. The reactions of the characters take over with sub-plots arising out of the main action — an accident — and the relationships between the people in the story.

Anita Brookner has published ten novels. Perhaps the best-known is

Hotel du Lac which won the prestigious Booker Prize. Her novels are not built around action-plots: they aren't filled with dramatic events. The plots of her novels are relatively simple, with women (and occasionally men) in emotional turmoil. Take a recent novel, *Fraud*. The story (told in about 100 000 words) is about Anna Durrant, a middle-aged woman, who after the death of her mother, goes missing. It's not a detective novel; we know that Anna is safely in Paris. The whole plot or story is about Anna's inner, reflective life and the attitude of friends to her and their views of her. What makes Anita Brookner's novels so special is not dramatic action but the emotions of unhappy people, described with grave, moving insights.

Activity

The plot is the story. Take a theme: it could be any one of these: an accident; a change of job; a new friend; a change of house and home; a journey or holiday event. They are just suggestions. The theme should be your theme. Make brief notes of the synopsis of the plot. The synopsis need not be more than 50 or 100 words but try to provide the whole picture.

Characters

Constructing the personalities of different people is a real test of the imagination. The skill in doing so marks out a good novelist from an indifferent one. Think of characters from novels that have become household names — Jane Eyre, Sherlock Holmes, David Copperfield, Horace Rumpole. It helps, of course, to remember characters such as these because the names are the titles of novels and films, or television series have been made about them. Here's a different test: can you name memorable characters whose names aren't titles (add to a list that could include Heathcliffe, Elizabeth Bennet, Long John Silver, James Bond.

Activity

Now pick out **three** people from novels that you remember well. In your notebook jot down the reasons why these characters stick in your memory. Your reasons will reflect the skill of the authors in constructing such people; therefore your notes should provide clues to the writing skills employed in character-construction.

Unreal people

Characters in a novel are not real people. They may be based on a person known to the author or, if the characters are set in historical novels, they may be based on research. But an author uses his or her imagination as well as research. This combination of close observation of people plus imaginative exaggeration creates the people that inhabit novels.

Giving life to your characters

A plot cannot exist without believable characters. Some of your characters may be near-perfect. But don't overdo the perfection. Jane Austen said of her heroine Anne Elliot in *Persuasion* that 'she is almost too good for me'. Constancy and integrity are fine virtues but it would be unreal if all the characters in a novel had these qualities. Nor should characters be wholly bad (but it's difficult to think well of serial killers such as Dr Hannibal Lecter in *Silence of the Lambs*). Another pitfall are stereotypes — clever professors, glib politicians, sensible mums, super-efficient who-looks-after-her-boss secretaries and so on. There may be people with these virtues but it's that daft Professor Branestawm that people remember and read about, not the sound, sensible academic professors.

People also change: a weak novel will have characters that react in the same way and are much the same kind of person at the end of the story that they were on page one. People alter with experience, especially if the experiences are dramatic.

Lastly, boring novels have characters who make obvious remarks or where people speak in stilted, predictable prose.

Activity

Having described the weaknesses of characters in novels, let's turn to the strengths. You've listed some fictional characters that have impressed you; now jot down in a notebook some of the factors that make people come alive. You'll have to re-read a few of your favourite novels to come up with some answers.

Libel

Your inspiration may be so startling that every character you invent is totally original. That's unlikely. Characters are based on people known to the writer. But what you must never do is name real people (or even a close approximation). Nor should you describe someone in such a way that he or she can be recognized. If you do, you could be liable for a libel action, especially if you have ridiculed your best friend Joan James who bears a striking resemblance to bitchy Janet Jones in your novel.

A second danger is to pick on a name (perhaps from the telephone book) and give this person an address. If the address or town is a real one, you could be in trouble. The way to avoid this danger is to check the voters' roll in the library for addresses (say Rose Street) and the names of people who live in this street. Better to be safe.

Similarly, avoid naming real famous people if they are alive. A critical word about a former prime minister or sports personality could bring an action for damages to their reputation.

Names, age and status

We all know who James Bond is. Would he have defeated Blofeld, Goldfinger and Dr No and would he have dazzled Miss Moneypenny if he'd been called Joe Bloggs or Fred Faggot? There is a famous Joe, Joe Lampton of *Room At the Top*, a Yorkshire lad aiming for social respectability; perhaps not as memorable if he'd been called Bertie Wooster.

Choose characters' names with care: they tell you about class, social milieu, geographical origin and hint at personality. Some writers (as John

Braine explains in *Writing a Novel*) jot down some details of each major character: age, origin, education, jobs, physical appearance, family and friends, children.

'With hair like over-cooked spaghetti'

How you dress people, and their life-style, is far more effective as a guide to character than long-winded character descriptions. And, if heroine Joanna Jessop enjoys cooking, readers don't want the benefit of all her favourite recipes.

There are some basic rules about dressing and possessing a character:

- Avoid stereotypes: all baddies aren't fat, have piggy eyes, and wear Armani suits.
- Get it right. If someone has a Ford Cavalier, you don't know your cars.
- Possessions (like actions) should add to knowledge of the character and be believable: it's possible that Betty and Bill Place, who have a fish shop, collect rare editions of Proust and Baudelaire, but it would be unusual.

There's a lot more to building characters in novels. To learn more about this art, you should read John Braine's *Writing a Novel*.

Activity

Now that you've learned a little about character, write 200 or so words to describe a character you would feature in your best-selling novel. The character could be descriptively constructed — face, clothes, stance, etc. — or it could emerge from conversation (dialogue).

When complete, ask someone to read and comment. Remember to avoid making the character too near someone you know.

Action, dialogue and description

At writing schools a regular question to tutors is on the balance that should be set between dialogue, action and description. An easy answer would be to say a third for each component. Easy but wrong. Wrong because it sounds like an inflexible rule. A more constructive answer is to say 'match the prescription to the patient', that is to decide whether dialogue will feature strongly or if it would be more appropriate to describe action rather than let characters talk their way through it.

Let's define these terms.

Action can be **descriptive writing**, **dialogue**, or a mixture of both. Descriptive language is framed so that the author **tells** the reader what is happening, or what a character looks like physically, or what he or she does. The action is therefore at a distance, as if a commentator was describing the scene and the players. The advantage of descriptive writing is that it allows for the full range of language — words, sentence-construction, paragraphing.

Dialogue is what people say to each other. They can also talk to themselves (the technical phrase is 'interior monologue'). Dialogue's advantages are the use of direct speech which brings pace and impact. A disadvantage is that the language may be limited (people don't generally make descriptive speeches to each other). The weakness of a novel is displayed in excessive — and irrelevant — dialogue, easily recognizeble as padding. Good dialogue stands the test of being read aloud.

Together, the mixture of description and dialogue gives the action in the story. Skilfully matched, they carry the narrative and character development on and on.

What's your style? What's your preference?

The answer is that both seem to satisfy reader-audiences. Long, blockbuster novels have both elements in profusion, especially family-history sagas. Thriller-writers prefer lean, terse, dialogue-driven novels.

Activity

Here's an example. Read this extract from *Wilt* by Tom Sharpe. What comments would you make about this brief exchange? The lines come from Chapter 1. Henry Wilt, 'not a decisive man' has spent 10 years seeking and failing to secure promotion from Lecturer (Grade Two) at his college. Eva Wilt, ambitious and energetic, likes to meet new people. At a flower show she bumps into Sally.

'I beg your pardon,' she said and turned to find herself looking into a pair of dark eyes.

'No need to apologize,' said the woman in an American accent. She was slight and dressed with a simple scruffiness that was beyond Eva Wilt's moderate income.

'I'm Eva Wilt,' said Eva, who had once attended a class on Getting to Know People at the Oakrington Village College. 'My husband lectures at the Tech and we live at 34 Parkview Avenue.'

'Sally Pringsheim.' said the woman with a smile. 'We're in Rossiter Grove. We're over on a sabbatical. Gaskell's a bio-chemist.'

Eva Wilt accepted the distinctions and congratulated herself on her perspicacity about the blue jeans and the sweater. People who lived in Rossiter Grove were a cut above Parkview Avenue and husbands who were biochemists on sabbatical were also in the University. Eva Wilt's world was made up of such nuances.

'You know, I'm not at all that sure I could live with an oratorical rose,' said Sally Pringsheim. 'Symphonies are OK in auditoriums but I can do without them in vases.'

Eva stared at her with a mixture of astonishment and admiration. To be openly critical of Mavis Mottram's flower arrangements was to utter blasphemy in Parkview Avenue. 'You know, I've always wanted to say that,' she said with a sudden surge of warmth, 'but I've never had the courage.'

Sally Pringsheim smiled, 'I think one should always say what one thinks. Truth is so essential in any really meaningful relationship. I always tell G baby exactly what I'm thinking.'

'Gee baby?' said Eva Wilt.

'Gaskell's my husband,' said Sally. 'Not that he's really a husband. It's just that we've got this open-ended arrangement for living together. Sure, we're legal and all that, but I think it's important sexually to keep one's options open, don't you?'

Every word counts

Among the points you may have noticed are:

1 The mixture of dialogue (short sentences, direct speech, no padding) with linked 'asides' in sharply phrased descriptive language, as in the 'No need to apologize' paragraph.
2 Tom Sharpe's brief and telling descriptions of Eva and Sally's clothes dress them as distinctive characters.
3 Their characters emerge, even in such a short episode: Eva warm, friendly, enthusiastic, slightly dotty; Sally cool, controlled, articulate.

Any other points?

Strong development: atmosphere and conflict

Let's suppose you have the **idea**, your **characters** are familiar to you, and the outline of the main **plot** is defined in your mind or in the draft notes. The skeleton of the novel is apparent.

The hard work now begins. Throughout the book, as it develops, the sub-plots carry the story forward; the characters have various adventures and meet other people, and so 'the plot thickens'.

Atmosphere surrounds the whole text: it could be mysterious, puzzling, amusing, frightening, challenging, historical, magical. And you have to decide whether the sub-plots are created by action or by people changing emotionally as a result of meeting other people.

Tools of the Trade, Part 2

There are several 'plotting tools' which can be learned.

1 An **event** is something that happens to a character. The happening could be external (such as a car crash) or internal (like falling in love). A plot depends on events. What can make a story interesting and readable is the way that your characters react to the event. Do they fear, love, despise, run — whatever they do carries the plot to the next stage.
2 **Stops on the line** means that a story has to be separated into stages, rather like stations on a railway line. The stops are the points reached in plot development. Time doesn't have to be chronological: you can jump forward and backwards in the time sequence, but of course, you must not make the mistake of giving people the wrong age or mix up events. Many authors construct a time-line on paper to show when things happened against time (year, month, week, day) scales.
3 **Climaxes** should occur at regular intervals. Agatha Christie was an expert at this technique, with murders spaced out, chapter by chapter. Other writers do it, too, perhaps more subtly.
4 **Sets** are more appropriate to making films. But they also apply to novels. A set is the historical or social milieu — and getting the details of time and place must be exact. For example, if your novel

is set in 1939, the clothes, food, newspaper stories and so on must all be accurate. Research is essential.

5 **Thesis, antithesis, synthesis** are philosophers' tools but can be just as appropriate for a novelist. They mean making a statement, then putting forward a counter-argument. Synthesis is the resolution of a solution from both: a device that is used to construct tension between characters.

6 **Conflicts** can be violent events or intellectual clashes. And if you feel the novel is wilting, introduce conflicts suddenly, with unusual consequences. This introduces a further concept — keep the reader in a state of **surprise**.

7 The relationships that develop between characters, interspersed with the action and conflict, create the **rhythm** of the novel. Language should quicken towards the end of the story. Another necessity is **segue** which is a technical word borrowed from music that describes the carry-over from one scene to another without pause. Lack of rhythm is shown in mechanical writing and paragraphs of the same length; lack of segue is demonstrated by scenes that seem to have no relevance to what's gone on before.

8 The **spiral of climaxes** is used in narrative fiction. It means the build up of events, conflicts and climaxes — to a final conclusion — The End. It's a technique used by most narrative fiction writers as a series of exciting, damaging or inspiring events or conflicts leading to a final climax. The phrase 'an anti-climax' is used to indicate someone's disappointment that nothing much happened — an anti-climax is a disaster for a novelist. Finally, then, end with a bang — unless you are deliberately writing a novel that peters out.

Putting it all together — viewpoint, style and The End

There are numerous books telling you how to write a novel. Some of the better ones are listed at the end of this book. One group of advisers or tutors will explain how to break down your concept for a story into chapters, how to sequence and pace them, how to build character, and so on. This approach is beneficial for aspiring beginner-writers. There's a craft to be learned.

Many beginners fail because when they sit down to write the novel they have clearly formulated in their minds, words fail them. The construction of, say, a 250 page book from a 'good idea' requires detailed preparation, plotting, drafting, re-writing, revising, despairing, triumphing over despair and persevering with other planning and emotional puzzles.

Writing is a craft. A full-fledged, active, professional writer can conceive the outline plot of a novel, carry these ideas in his or her head, and write it in one continuous sweep. This skill separates the professional from the amateur. Somewhere between the ambitious but unskilled amateur and the cool professional lies a dangerous field of play where many beginners surrender: they don't have the confidence, or the skills, or the determination to proceed. In short, they never reach The End.

Overcoming these hazards requires a mix of determination and mastery of the tools of the trade. These tools have been described — the concept, theme or idea; characters; plots and sub-plots; character-generated plots that lead to conflict, action and changing relationships between characters; the skilful use of language; the build-up of atmosphere, and so on. The mastery of these skills is essential and can be practised as you write. If they aren't grasped, then it's unlikely that a beginner-writer will ever reach The End and may be deterred from ever starting again.

This book is not a deterrent. It is intended to be constructive in assisting the development of writing skills for various purposes — in this case novel-writing. The positive purpose is to encourage people to write, polishing their skills as they proceed.

Through persistence and perseverance (qualities that are also needed when dealing with a publisher) you may complete your novel. Two of the major factors that will influence a publisher are style and viewpoint.

Style is a personal thing. The English language allows for an amazing variety of personal styles of writing — the prolix, the profane, the succinct, spoken-word commentary, poetic description, journalistic. Your style is an extension of you — it reflects your views on life, your background reading and education, your interests and enthusiasms, and your writing craft. Think for a moment of any group of six contemporary women novelists: Anita Brookner, Iris Murdoch, P. D. James, Joanna Trollope, Jilly Cooper, Barbara Taylor Bradford. They all have vastly different **styles**.

Activity

Choose a different group of six novelists. Jot down their names. Then spend a few minutes in reflecting and then writing down in your own words the differences that you detect in their various **styles** of writing.

Viewpoint

Viewpoint is your own particular voice. If people ask 'What is the book about?' — that's viewpoint. It's partly the story. It's more the personal point of view expressed by the writer. It is a combination of all the factors — plot, characters, description, dialogue, action, moral or social views, style. It is what distinguishes, say, one crime novel from another — Elmore Leonard from Ruth Rendell, Conan Doyle from Ellis Peters, Agatha Christie from Dick Francis.

Viewpoint answers another question, 'What does this novel *say?*' This means its political, social or personal stance. For example, contemporary novels may have a theme where the author indicates his or her view of contemporary problems such as poverty, injustice, illness, single-parents, unemployment, crime and punishment, good triumphing over evil.

The next time you read a novel try to detect the author's view on the theme of the novel. The viewpoint may, of course, be skilfully disguised but characters have to say something, and this is where the clues lie.

Activity

Let's look at one example only. This extract is from an unusual modern, best-selling book. *Restoration* by Rose Tremain is about Robert Merivel who abandons his medical studies to indulge in gluttony, indolence and foolishness at the Court of King Charles II. The book which is intelligent, imaginative, funny and gripping, demonstrates the fusion of all the elements of novel-writing that have been analysed. This extract, from the first chapter, is Robert Merivel's description of himself. Having read it, consider and write a few lines on how you view:

1   Character
2   Style and viewpoint.

'I don't know whether you can imagine me yet. I am thirty-seven years old as this year, 1664, moves towards its end. My stomach is large and also freckled, although it has seldom been exposed to the sun. It looks as if a flight of minute moths had landed on it in the night. I am not tall, but this is the age of the high heel. I strive to be particular about my clothes, but am terribly in the habit of dropping morsels of dinner on them. My eyes are blue and limpid. In childhood, I was considered angelic and was frequently buttoned inside a suit of blue moiré, thus seeming to my mother a little world entire: sea and sand in my colours, and the lightness of air in my baby voice. She went to her fiery death still believing that I was a person of honour. In the scented gloom of Amos Treefeller's back room (the place of all our private conversations), she would take my hand and whisper her hopes for my splendid future. What she couldn't see, and what I had not the heart to point out, was that we no longer live in an honourable age. What has dawned instead is the Age of Possibility. And it is only the elderly (as my mother was) and the truculently myopic (as my friend Pearce is) who haven't noticed this and are not preparing to take full advantage of it. Pearce, I am ashamed to admit, fails to understand, let alone laugh at, the jokes from Court I feel obliged to relay to him on his occasional visits to me from his damp Fenland house. The excuse he made is that he's a Quaker. This, in turn, makes me laugh.

. . . So this is how you might imagine me: at table, rustling with laughter in a gaudy suit, my migrant hair flattened by a luxuriant wig, my freckles powered, my eyes twinkling in the candlelight, my pudding being ejected from my mouth by that force within me which snorts at sobriety and is so greedy for foolishness. Do not flatter yourself that I am elegant or worthy in any way, but yet I am, at this moment that you glimpse me, a rather popular man. I am also in the middle of story which might have a variety of endings, some of them not entirely to my liking.'

© Rose Tremain, 1989

Summary

In this unit you have looked briefly at some of the complexities involved in writing a novel.

What you should — or might — have learned from it is

- the need to read published novels (especially novels of some quality) more carefully to analyse their component parts
- the importance of planning which involves first writing a story synopsis, brief notes on the main characters and the sequence of sub-plots that will carry the story forward in a paced sequence
- how relationships between people in novels create atmosphere and action, and how conflict is a major factor in determining plot-development.

Assignment 6

To be attempted after completing Unit 12.
Time guide: 4 hours

The Novel

You will be relieved to learn that the final assignment is not to write a novel. You can, of course, write one if you wish.

But to be more realistic, this assignment is on the preparation for and some aspects of novel-writing.

1   Start with the **theme** or **concept**. Explain in a few lines what the novel is to be about — perhaps a love story, perhaps a family story, women fighting against family or personal difficulties; or it could be a crime, mystery, western or other kind of novel.

2   Map out briefly the **plot** of the novel. Write a synopsis of about a page at least, possibly more, to explain how the story will develop, with a beginning, middle and end.

3   List and describe some of the **characters** in the novel. Concentrate on their personal characteristics learning from character-definitions such as Robert Merivel in *Restoration* or in other novels you have enjoyed.

4   Take one example of **action**, **conflict** or **atmosphere** and write a page or paragraph illustrating one of these factors.

5   Finally, write the first or last chapter of your best-seller. Length could be up to, say, 3000 words.

When you have completed Assignment 6, ask a friend, or a member of your family or a tutor to read and comment on it.

UNIT 13 PUBLISHING: PREPARING FOR PUBLICATION

Objectives

When you have completed this unit you should be able to:
- prepare a manuscript for submission to a publisher
- understand some of the processes of editing and of the production procedures that are required to produce a book or magazine
- appreciate some of the commercial and financial aspects of publishing.

The publishing business

You may not want your writing to go any further than a private view or your bottom drawer. That is, you are quite happy to write for yourself, family and friends. If so, you don't need to study this unit.

However, you may have open or secret ambitions to be published. This means that as well as being a writer you need to be in sales and marketing. You have to sell your ideas, your article or your manuscript to a publisher who will spend time, money and patience in an effort to make a commercial profit from your efforts.

Publishing is a business. Editors' time is costed. No editor can spare his or her precious, expensive time to teach you how to write or how to prepare your copy for publication. Therefore, in the same way that you would prepare for a job interview, you need to prepare your manuscript for a warm welcome in a busy publisher's office.

Activity

Put yourself in an editor's position. If you were a magazine or book editor receiving articles and manuscripts relentlessly by each post, what qualities in the presentation of material would impress you? Jot down your ideas.

Know your business

Your answer should contain some of these points, and others that might occur to you:

1 **It is the correct destination?**
Publishers' lists should be examined to see if they publish the kind of material you've written. Don't send poetry to a non-fiction publisher, or your blockbuster novel to a company that hasn't a

fiction list. Amazingly, shots in the dark occur; many authors simply don't do their homework.

2 **Quality, not quantity**

A publisher doesn't take kindly to the arrival out of the blue of a substantial parcel of a 700 or so page manuscript. A preliminary letter is wise, with a synopsis, and up to three or four chapters. For a magazine article or short story, the complete story can be sent. For a novel the covering letter should ask if the publisher would like to read the whole work.

3 **Singles, not multiples**

An editor hates receiving a letter and copy that has been clearly duplicated for despatch to multiple addresses. We all enjoy a personal approach. One tip is to use the telephone to find out from the target publisher the name of the particular commissioning editor likely to receive your letter and copy (that is, children's, fiction, travel or other specialism).

4 **Smart, not tatty**

If you were an editor, you wouldn't want to read handwritten copy. Careful preparation of your copy before despatch is essential, and this aspect is described later in this unit. Nor should the typewritten pages look as if they have been sent to and returned from a dozen other publishers. Send clean, photocopied pages that look pristine and purposeful.

5 **Pay now, not later**

Magazine and book editors complain about the arrival of unwanted manuscripts, without payment for their return. It may seem mean to an author, but publishers are conscious of their costs, so to ensure a safe return, enclose a large envelope with sufficient stamps.

These are some answers; did you think of others?

Find yourself a publisher

From the hundreds of book publishing companies and the 900 or so titles registered as magazines, how do you select the right target?

The answer is, as it has been all through this book, research.

There are two vital sources. The *Writers' & Artists' Yearbook*, published annually by A & C Black and available in bookshops and libraries, lists UK newspapers and magazines, with addresses and telephones and a few lines to indicate their field. A typical category entry for a magazine is 'holidays and health, fashion and food, finance and fiction, hobbies and home; length 600 to 1200 words; payment: £100 per 1000 words'. The *Yearbook* lists UK book publishers, with a similar factual entry of name, address, telephone, fax, named senior managers, categories of publishing — 'food and wine, theatre, playscripts, travel guides'. There are substantial sections on overseas publishers; markets for radio and television screenplays; agents; freelance editorial services; music, photography and other media publishers; and general articles.

Another very useful book is *The Writers' Handbook* edited by Barry Turner, published by Macmillan.

One or both of these books should be acquired by a writer; as well as the target details, they contain expert advice on the preparation of a manuscript.

> ## Activity
>
> You must by now have some idea of the category, field or genre that you'd like to specialize in. Consult one of the two books listed above (or any other source you think is appropriate) and find out the names, addresses and other facts about three possible targets for your work. Draft a letter that you would send along with your article, story or synopsis.

Find an agent

A direct approach to an editor or publishing company is usually the best way to proceed. However, once established, most writers employ a literary agent to administer their business.

Why?

Agents are experts. (Well, the vast majority are; there are muddlers in every business).

They are expert in:

- Writing: they read so many manuscripts (and have often been editors themselves) that they know immediately if a manuscript is well written. If not, they may offer advice.
- Targets: they are expert in knowing the specialisms of different publishers and won't make the mistake of sending it to a wrong one.
- Business: literary agents have wide experience of terms — advances, royalties, contracts, and so will negotiate the best deal they can on your behalf. They will also negotiate the sale of US, translation, dramatic, film and all other rights.

But:

There are several 'buts'!

- An agent won't take you on unless you've already been published (that is, you are the author of a published novel, short stories, poems, plays, articles). For a beginner, it's Catch 22: you need an agent to persuade a publisher to take your work but you can't get an agent until you've been published.
- Agents levy commissions on your work - usually 10 per cent of gross income. If an agent tries to charge more than 15 per cent, go elsewhere.
- Agents are not there to teach people how to write. They do not have the time to advise on unsuitable manuscripts.
- Agents are busy people: as well as being unwilling to take on newcomers, they can be just as dilatory as publishers.

To find an agent, consult the *Writers' & Artists' Yearbook* which indicates specialisms. A preliminary letter is essential to see if an agent will consider you as a potential client.

Contracts and conditions

Let's suppose the sun shines. A letter arrives. With it is a contract.

Most contracts are based on an agreed pattern. Writers' groups such as the Society of Authors offer advice on how to read and interpret contracts.

The main terms specify the publisher's requirement that the manuscript should be delivered by a certain date and in a certain form, such as 'typed or printed out from a word processing system on A4 paper, double-spaced, with margins of at least three centimetres top and bottom, left and right'.

Other requirements may be that the author provides illustrations; agrees to read and mark proofs by an agreed date (with penalties if deadlines are not met); and that the author obtains written permissions for the use of copyright materials.

Financial terms are also specified: they can be as low as 5 per cent of the cover price for a new author; more usually 10 per cent; and up to 15 per cent for famous big sellers. Subsidiary rights have to be watched. The publisher will demand the right to license for a paperback edition; if so 50 or 60 per cent of royalty income is acceptable. Translation and foreign language rights, and book club rights are generally demanded by the publisher, but the royalty should be specified. Along with royalty, there should be an advance on sales; take it, and even ask for more, because it's possible that your book will be a slow seller, so at least you had some money 'up front'.

Tied hand and foot

The answer is, don't sign it. This is the famous 'option clause' which doesn't give you an option. It is virtually unenforceable in law, and it ties an author to a publisher who may be good but could be very, very bad.

Remember that a publisher hasn't purchased anything from an author: the contract is a licence to trade in an author's originality. On the other hand, you won't be published until you do sign a contract.

Preparation of copy

Some advice has already been given for the preparation of a manuscript
- typed, not handwritten
- neat, not tatty.

There are further considerations.

Typed or word processed?

Increasingly, authors are using word processors. For publishers, there are two big advantages: a disk can be acquired and the printout is likely (if the correct computer instructions have been made) to be A4, with correct margins and on clean paper. The copy editor who works on a manuscript can thus make corrections, stylistic or house-style changes on screen by using your disk or on clean printed copy.

If the manuscript is to be **typed**, there are some conventions to note and apply. If you apply these rules, you'll make a most favourable impression on the publisher.

- Use the black ribbon. For plays, use capitals for character names and underline stage directions.
- Paper should be standard size A4 typewriter paper. Type on one side of the paper only.
- Margins should be generous, especially on the left. A margin of 3 cm left and right is acceptable.
- All typed text should be double spaced. This is essential to allow for an editor's changes.
- Don't vary your spelling of the same word! For instance, 'z' has generally replaced 's' in 'organisation', so don't use both, and there are many other examples.
- Number all pages consecutively; if extra pages (the technically correct word is 'folios') are required later, make the new one 52A, and write on the bottom of page 52 'folio 52A follows'. But don't make a habit of it.
- Don't have your manuscript bound. A ring-binder is best. Don't staple the pages, leave them as virgin territory.

Marking up, proofs and corrections

When a manuscript ('typescript' means the same thing) is received and a contract is signed, there is likely to be a gap of two or three months. An efficient publisher will tell you what's happening.

Generally what occurs is that the manuscript is 'read'. This means that an editor in-house or a freelance editor or adviser out-house will read and comment, and may suggest alterations. Your manuscript (and/or disk) may then be returned with a request to consider and make changes.

At the next stage a copy editor will 'mark-up' the copy. This means that the technical information needed by a typesetter will be added. An author isn't involved in this process.

Once 'set' in the format of the printed page (with or without illustrations) the author will next see his or her work in the form of a 'proof'. Most books and magazines are now produced with only one set of proofs, whereas in the past there were two. The reasons are of cost.

Proofs come in various forms. One may be a computer print-out: the copy is the same as a printed page but it looks a lot different at proof stage. The most likely form is a laser print of a page — these are **page**

proofs and are the nearest thing to the finished article. They include page numbers, headlines, illustrations.

As an author you will be asked to 'check the proofs'. This isn't an invitation to re-write. Indeed your contract will have contained a statement (which you've signed) that 'alterations in proof by the author (with corrections of typesetters and the publisher's editors excepted) which exceed 10 per cent of the manuscript shall be at the cost of the author.'

And costs can be high: a comma or full stop can be charged.

Into production

Once proofs are returned, the author's job is finished. You may be asked to help with the copy needed for advertising and catalogue material, such as details of your background and career. All other tasks are the publisher's. These include the assembly of text and illustrations, the reproduction of photographs, printing and binding. The contract specifies how many free copies are given to an author (generally six). A helpful editor will keep an author informed of progress; if not, the pleasant surprise comes with the arrival of six copies and a cheque (if the contract includes an advance payable on publication).

Review activity

There is a technical language with symbols to tell a typesetter or printer the precise requirements of an editor. When copy is 'marked up', information is of two kinds: instructions on headlines, indents (spaces), typeface and typesize, etc. The other information is of alterations to the text itself.

When editors correct copy, they use a system of symbols. Some of them are shown opposite.

This is an exercise in copy preparation.

There are errors and inconsistencies in this piece of copy. Correct it. That is, mark it up so that it is consistent and free of errors. For instance, correct the spelling (typing!) errors. Mark up the start of paragraphs by using the indent from the mark up symbols guide that is provided. Add the title. Show where commas, full stops, colons, semi-colons, apostrophes should go. Indicate letter spaces, close up on unnecessary spaces and indicate capitals.

Apart from its value as an activity-assignment, the article describes most graphically the problems faced by a writer-at-home.

An Office At Home

'At twenty minutes to seven the first alarm goes off. I need two alarms In between them I doze, half asleep, waiting for the second call. But my son usually bats me to it; I hear the toilet or the shower and sit up, trying to get my brain in gear for the day a head.

Half an hour later William crashes out of the front door to catch the school bus. At about this time my daughter appears. So too does the post there's a flood of it because two weeks' ago I was on a phone in radio programme and made some remarks many people didn't like. The result — for every letter of approval there's ten of hate-mail.

MARK UP SYMBOLS

The most common mark up symbols used by editors are as follows:

Instruction	Symbol	Example
Insert a word (or letter)	⅄	This is t̯e end
Delete (take out)	⌿	This is the⌿ end
Transpose (adjacent letters/words)	⎍	This ⟨the⟨is⟩end
Substitute	/ or ___	Th⟋s is the end or end This is the beginning
Delete and close up	⌢̮	To⌿day
Close up (remove space)	⌢̮	Pub ⌢ lisher
Begin new paragraph	⌐	the end. ⌐The beginning
Run on (no paragraph)	⌇	the end. ⌇ The beginning of the next
Set in lower case	/	This is ⟋he ⟋nd
Set in capitals	≡	This is the end
Set in small capitals	≣	This is the end
Set in italic type	___	This is the end
Set in bold type	∿	This is the end
Centre in the line	⊏ ⊐	⌈Heading⌉
Set flush left	⊐	⌉Flush left
Set flush right	⊏	Flush right ⌐
Indent	⊐	⌈First sentence . . .
No indent (full out)	⊢—	⊢——First sentence
Ignore this mark	⊘	Do not make this correction
Full point	⊙	the end⊙
Comma	⌃	the middle⌃the end⊙
Semi colon (colon)	⊙; (⊙:)	a break in the middle; or as follows:
Apostrophe	⌇	Publisher⟋s· office
Insert space between words	Ⴤ	This is⌣he end
Reduce space between words	⌇	This ⌇ is the end

109

Without an office or an in-tray I put some letters aside to answer at a later date. I've done this many times and haven't yet found the missing letters. I once made a good resolution — answer mail straight away; don't let it pile up. It was a good idea and lasted until about January 15th. The second solution was to put a day aside for letter-answering; if I didn't the mountan would overwhelm us. But I'm notorious for putting off the day — next week, sometime, never.

An office, then? An office of my own? I read an article about a 'famous author' who has his own super-model word processor, can cope with E-mail and has a call-in secretary. Such grandeur. In my house there's no pros pect of an office. I though a filing cabinet would help and bought one at an auction: it's now in the garage with the lawnmower.

By nine o'clock the house is quiet. Son and daughter have gone. Once upstairs, I move into my office. Some people would call it a bedroom. It's a short walk to the exective desk, just a step around the bed, actually. I make the bed because I stack papers in neat piles on the duvet.

As a novelist I need a run of two or three times at the word processor (mine is an elderly Amstrad). To avoid snarling up the printer, I hook up the curtains so they don't jam in the mechanism; the curtain has to be fiddled so that the sun doesn't shine on the screen.

Now I'm ready, awaiting inspiration. Writers have many different ways of conjuring up ideas: my way is to read yesterday's pages, altering a word here and there, perhaps re-writing a paragraph. For me, this is enough — the story begins to flow in my mind and fingers get to work.

Next, concentration. I find that 30 minutes is enough: I stand up, stretch, walk through the house, touch my toes a dozen times. Sitting at a word processor continuously gives me cramp heaven knows what damage is being done to my back. Physical exercise, therefore, is a necessity. Then back to work for another thirty minutes.

Thats my working routine. The office is a table in a small bedroom. Even so, despite these limitations, I can work. Cramped in my office, I've written a radio play, a novel,, three short stories — all published, too — and a novel. All-in two years. The radiowork comes from guest appearance on talks' programmes: it's amazing how one extravagant remark can lead to another invitation to next week's programme.

At lunch time I let the printer loose, first making sure there's enough paper. A light lunch, followed either by a snooze in the chair or a swift walk across the park. But by two o'clock I'm in the office chair again. (That's one extravagance — I bought a good chair, taking pity on my back).

When school finishes, I finish. Evenings are for my children: Dad cleared off three years ago and although they have their own social and sporting lives, I make sure that I'm a permanent reserve, 'super-sub' as my son puts it, in one of his kinder remarks.

I read somewhere about a famous author who leaves home, traveles to an office, and writes to the same disciplines as if he's working as an accountant. Such luxury! I'd settle for a spare bedroom but in our terrace house there's only three for three of us. One day, perhaps, a novel will turn into a best seller and we can move to set me up in the grandeur of an accountant's office; until then, the relentless green face of the Amstrad stares at me, shrouded by elderly Liura Ashley curtains.

This is the end!'

Read all about it

If you would like to know more about book and magazine publishing, there are some good books. Among them are:

Copyediting by Judith Butcher, Cambridge University Press, 3rd edition, 1992: it's essential for an author on points of style and consistency.
Inside Book Publishing by Giles Clark, Blueprint, 1994 describes the business of book publishing.
Inside Magazines by Michael Barnard, Blueprint, 1994, does a similar job for magazine publishing.
Finding Out About Printing by Ivor Powell and Alan Jamieson, Hobsons, 1989 is a simple guide to the various stages of book and magazine production.

Summary

In this unit you have been introduced to the main aspects of publishing, seen from an author's viewpoint. You should have increased your knowledge and understanding of a publisher's relationship with and needs from an author in terms of:

- contract terms
- employing an agent
- manuscript preparation.

Having completed the various activities you should also have improved your skills in manuscript preparation and presentation and thus — depending on the worthiness of your writing — have made yourself a more attractive proposition to a publisher.

APPENDIX
FURTHER READING

Some of these books have already been mentioned or recommended in the text. There are also other books which you should find useful. If you wish to study creative writing, book and magazine production and the business of publishing in greater depth, you will find them all valuable for every one has different points to make.

General
Writers' & Artists' Yearbook, A & C Black
John Fairfax and John Moat, *The Way to Write*, Elm Tree Books
Ann Hoffman, *Research for Writers*, A & C Black
Barry Turner, *The Writers' Handbook*, Macmillan

Magazines and newspapers
Morag Campbell, *Writing About Travel*, A & C Black
Jill Dick, *Freelance Writing for Newspapers*, A & C Black
Jill Dick, *Writing for Magazines*, A & C Black

Children
Joan Aiken, *The Way to Write for Children*, Elm Tree Books
Margaret Clark, *Writing for Children*, A & C Black
Ann de Gale, *Writing for the Teenage Market*, A & C Black
David Silwyn Williams, *How to Write for Teenagers*, Allison and Busby

Plays and poetry
Brad Ashton, *How to Write Comedy*, Elm Tree Books
Michael Baldwin, *The Way to Write Poetry*, Elm Tree Books
Steve Gooch, *Writing a Play*, A & C Black
Stuart Griffiths, *How Plays Are Made*, Elm Tree Books

Radio and television
William Ash, *The Way to Write Radio Drama*, Elm Tree Books
Gordon Croton, *From Script to Screen*, BBC
Rosemary Horstmann, *Writing for Radio*, A & C Black
Gerald Kelsey, *Writing for Television*, A & C Black
Norman Longmate, *Writing for the BBC*, BBC
Eric Paice, *The Way to Write for Television*, Elm Tree Books
Andrew Popperwell and Michael Kaye, *Making Radio*, BBC

Novels and short stories
Michael Baldwin, *The Way to Write Short Stories*, Elm Tree Books
John Braine, *Writing a Novel*, Eyre Methuen
Christopher Dolley, editor, *The Penguin Book of English Short Stories*, Penguin
André Jute, *Writing a Thriller*, A & C Black
H. R. F. Keating, *Writing Crime Fiction*, A & C Black

Paddy Kitchen, *The Way to Write Novels*, Elm Tree Books

Publishing

Michael Barnard, *Inside Magazines*, Blueprint
Judith Butcher, *Copyediting*, Cambridge University Press
Giles Clark, *Inside Book Publishing*, Blueprint

INDEX